UNLIKELY ALLIES

UNLIKELY ALLIES

The Christian-Socialist Convergence

Gary MacEoin

CROSSROAD • NEW YORK

1990

The Crossroad Publishing Company
370 Lexington Avenue, New York, NY 10017

Printed in the United States of America
Typesetting output: TEXSource, Houston

Library of Congress Cataloging-in-Publication Data

MacEóin, Gary, 1909-
    Unlikely allies : the Christian-socialist convergence / Gary
MacEoin.
      p. cm.
    Includes bibliographical references.
    ISBN 0-8245-1046-1
    1. Socialism, Christian.   2. Socialism and Christianity.
I. Title.
HX51.M33 1990
335'.7 — dc20   90-33871
                                         CIP

Contents

Preface

Socialism as a serious political challenger to the capitalist organization of society dates from the middle of the nineteenth century. Although everywhere legally, morally, and ecclesiastically condemned, it succeeded in becoming institutionalized, in a mere hundred years, in sovereign states in Europe, Asia, Africa, and America, so that governments identifying themselves as socialist now rule more than a third of humankind.

In a typical dictionary entry, socialism is described as "a theory or system of social organization which advocates the vesting of the ownership and control of the means of production, capital, land, etc., in the community as a whole."[1] There are, however, wide variations in the use of the word. The minimal requirements for a theory or system to be called socialist would seem to be the control in the public interest of the major means of production. That control might be exercised in various ways, such as cooperatives or worker councils, with a supervisory role for the state to protect the community interest. All existing socialist states identify themselves as Marxist-inspired. In all of them, the state plays a dominant role as owner and operator of the means of production, including the communications media.

Even before the middle of the nineteenth century, elements within the Christian churches advocated various forms of socialism out of pastoral concern for members of their community reduced to subhuman living conditions as workers in industry. These churches as institutions, however, always supported the established social order, and their opposition to change increased with the rise of militant movements committed to the violent overthrow of governments and the radical restructuring of society, movements

vii

that drew their inspiration from the ideas of Karl Marx. This institutional opposition not only continued into the twentieth century but actually increased in its second quarter when church leaders joined with the governments of capitalist countries in focusing on atheism as an integral element of Marxism and thus an insurmountable obstacle for all people who believe in God.

After the middle of the twentieth century, however, significant changes began on both sides. What had seemed a monolithic Marxist bloc, controlled by the Soviet Union, began a process of decentralization and the formation of at least relatively autonomous groupings. Until recently, nevertheless, all these regimes followed more or less faithfully the political forms and ideological attitudes developed in the Soviet Union after the October Revolution of 1917. This involved the monopoly of power by a single party, a centrally planned economy, severe limitations on freedom of expression and movement, identification of the state as professedly atheistic, restrictions on the practice of religion, at times to the level of open persecution, and aggressive propagation of atheism.

This apparently solid political structure began in the late 1980s to crumble unexpectedly and with surprising rapidity in the Soviet Union and in the nations of Eastern Europe over which the Soviet Union had exercised hegemony since the end of World War II. Everywhere, critical voices were allowed to challenge officialdom. The monopoly of power enjoyed by the Communist Party was openly protested. Some countries recognized other parties and authorized them to compete for power in open elections. Formal recognition of the right to freedom of religious belief and practice was affirmed, and the believer was guaranteed full equality as a citizen where legal or administrative restrictions had existed. With the sole exception of Romania, these radical changes were effected without significant violent resistance.

December 1989 opened with an official visit of President Mikhail S. Gorbachev to the Vatican, where he was received with elaborate protocol. Pope John Paul II welcomed the meeting as providing an opportunity to expand the collaboration of the Catholic church and the Soviet Union in a common commitment to peace and worldwide cooperation. Our meeting, he added, "is extraordinarily meaningful as a sign of the times that have slowly matured, a sign that is rich in all it promises." In his reply, Gorbachev affirmed the right of all Soviet citizens "to satisfy their spiritual needs," stressed the common interest and common concern of the Soviet Union and the Vatican in promoting European solidarity, and announced that the pope and he had agreed in principle to establish formal relations between the two states.

In a separate speech to a Roman audience during the same visit, Gorbachev further insisted that religion has "a positive potential" in the task of creating the new man and the new society. "We have ceased to claim a monopoly of truth," he said, "and we no longer insist that we are the best or that we are always right. And if people don't agree with us, we don't treat them as enemies. In politics, we are now firmly and irreversibly guided by the principle of freedom of choice; in economics, science, and technology, by the principle of reciprocal benefit; in spiritual and ideological matters, by the principle of dialogue and of openness to everything that is applicable to our situation. . . . We recognize that faith is not only a problem of the individual conscience with which nobody should interfere, but also that the moral values that religion has developed and transmitted can and do also serve the cause of the renewal of our country."[2]

Long before these events, the monolithic rejection of socialism by the Christian churches, both Catholic and Protestant, had begun to break down. While as institutions they generally kept their distance, many of their members began to face the fact of socialist control of much of the world and to seek ways for coexistence. By the mid-1960s Christian missionaries in all parts of the Third World were challenging the capitalist system as incapable of providing human living conditions for two-thirds of the world's inhabitants and asserting that the only viable alternative at the present juncture of human affairs was some form of socialism.

These scattered church advocates of socialism discovered they had a much stronger base than they suspected when in 1970 the people of Chile chose a Marxist president to lead their country by constitutional means to socialism. Almost overnight there developed a substantial movement of Christians for Socialism not only in Chile but in most countries with a significant Christian population. Simultaneously, for the first time since the sixteenth-century

Reformation, Catholic and Protestant theologians joined in developing a theology. This theology of liberation stressed the Christian commitment to a special option for the poor and to active participation in the task of creating here on earth a society that would provide for all its members the opportunity to develop their human potential. Almost without exception, liberation theologians have adopted a Marxist analysis as a tool for interpreting the reality in which they live.

Deep divisions exist within the Christian churches as to the possibility of reconciliation of Marxist socialism with Christian beliefs. There are legitimate grounds for such differences of opinion, especially because — contrary to popular myth — Marxism contains as many diverse positions as does Christianity itself. Conflict, however, often results, not from objective incompatibility of views, but from distortions sedulously cultivated by interested parties.

As is clear from Pope John Paul's comments to President Gorbachev, the extraordinary recent changes in Central Europe open up new possibilities for better relations between Christians and socialists. The image of a monolithic Marxism, a single orthodoxy functioning as a pseudo-religion, is irrevocably gone. But beyond that, what do the changes really mean? Violently contrasting interpretations of their significance have been put forward. For some, they demonstrate the failure of socialism to deliver on its utopian promises and constitute an affirmation of the validity of capitalism as the only economic system able to deliver the goods and services demanded by the global consumer.

For others, on the contrary, they reveal the strength of a system that can publicly rectify errors made during the period of bureaucratic centralization, a centralization that may have been necessary while weak socialist states battled for survival under economic — and often military — attack of hostile capitalism. In this interpretation, the changes reflect not weakness but robust growth and a willingness to compete with capitalism on its own terms.

Others again, applying evolutionary concepts to the social sphere, point out that the development of a new species involves many abortive attempts before a successful result is attained. In historic terms, socialism is still in its infancy. It took capitalism several centuries to establish itself worldwide, Gorbachev told his

Italian listeners, and the process involved "bloody revolutions, terrible wars, depressions, and other upheavals, even Fascism."[3]

Whatever the ultimate outcome of the recent changes in Eastern Europe, it will in all likelihood take a lifetime or two to determine whether the socialism that President Gorbachev continues to profess and promote has or does not have a future. In addition, we must continue to live with closed socialist regimes not only in China but in many other countries of Asia and Africa, not to mention the island of Cuba only ninety miles from the U.S. mainland. The current fluid situation in the socialist world makes it doubly important for Christians to understand what they have in common with socialists, and to determine if what separates them must prevent joining — as Pope John Paul proposed to President Gorbachev — in a common effort for peace and worldwide cooperation.

This book is offered as a starting point. It is an attempt to set out the pertinent facts and thus facilitate logical and informed discussion. It does not attempt to obscure the real differences, but it does try to identify them and distinguish them from the many distortions that bedevil much debate.

The book opens with an account of the evolution of modern socialism, with the Enlightenment and the French Revolution as its intellectual sources, and the emergence of industrial capitalism in Western Europe as its historic context. It develops the reasons why the major Christian churches committed themselves to support a capitalist system that at no time could objectively claim to stand for Christian principles. It stresses the polemical character of the major statements on both the Marxist and the Christian side, an attitude tending to exaggeration and distortion of the enemy's position rather than an effort to understand it. And with the theology of liberation in the second half of the twentieth century, the underlying story of the struggle of the powerless and voiceless becomes evident. One can see, from the Enlightenment to the present day, the gradual flowering of self-understanding and assumption of power by the masses who are finally emerging as the agents of history.

I believe that the subject is of central importance in our time. Supporters of the status quo certainly think so, devoting enormous effort to their project of delegitimating Marxism as an option for

Christians. Will Christianity consume itself by devoting its efforts for the rest of the century to justifying a capitalism that has demonstrated its inability to satisfy the basic needs of humans now living, to say nothing of the far greater numbers projected in the next fifty years? Or will it reassert its autonomy vis-à-vis the state so that it can proclaim the good news to the postcapitalist society that is already on the horizon? The issue seems to me that simple — and that ultimate.

Over the past several years the media in the United States and other capitalist countries have described in great detail the vast changes in the major socialist countries, from the Soviet Union's *glasnost* and *perestroika* to the massacres of students in Beijing's Tiananmen Square. These are indeed historic events and merit worldwide attention. I do not, however, share the common interpretation of these events as establishing that socialism has been tried and failed. What has failed is the dictatorial approach, the Lenin-Stalin attempt to impose from the top down. What we are witnessing here, I believe, is an upsurge from the base. It is analogous to what has been experienced by the Catholic church: Vatican I, papal infallibility; Vatican II, People of God (leading to Christian base communities). Of course, there is resistance both in church and in society to such radical changes. Power holders do not yield gracefully. The distorted interpretation of the changes offered by the media serves the interests of the power holders.

The analogy of what has happened in the Catholic church seems to me particularly relevant to what is happening in the Soviet Union and China. As the level of education, awareness, and sense of power of the laity grew, so did the pressures for greater participation and recognition in the community. Similarly, the success of socialist systems in achieving more equitable distribution of the national product, providing for the masses food, clothing, shelter, health services, and education, is creating explosive pressures. I think it will become increasingly clear that the present unrest does not mark a desire to return to capitalism but rather a demand to implement the missing elements in the socialist promise.

If my evaluation is correct, we can anticipate several years of turmoil in the socialist world, especially in China, the Soviet Union, Poland, and Hungary. They will be discussing in public the nature of socialism, a discussion in which all of us will join. One positive result already is the demise of the myth that Marxism is monolithic.

I began work on this project in 1974 when the Christians for Socialism movement was in the headlines. In 1978, for a variety of reasons, I was forced to suspend it. In 1988, however, I was invited to spend six months as St. Edmund's College, University of Cambridge, as Von Hügel Visiting Fellow and Writer in Residence at the Von Hügel Institute. There I had access to the vast library resources of the University of Cambridge and also of London. I further had the opportunity to go to Rome and obtain a printout of the hundreds of pertinent documents in the computers of IDOC Internazionale and to use the library of *Civiltà Cattolica*, a library that contains every book submitted for review to the premier Jesuit weekly since it began publication in 1850.

Many people contributed to making this book a reality. They include Diana Calafati, who as editor at a New York publisher first suggested the idea to me and who (now living in Rome) edited the finished work, Betsy Cohn, an indefatigable researcher and creative collaborator for four months in Cambridge, Richard Senier, William Wipfler, Peter Hinde, Elmer and Patti Sitkin, St. Mark's Presbyterian Church (Tucson) and its founding pastor, David Sholin, John Fife, and the Von Hügel Institute.

I have given an English-language source, whenever available, for quoted materials. Translations are mine for citations from languages other than English.

Chapter 1

The Age-Old Socialist Dream

"Socialism" and "communism" are terms that are frequently used interchangeably to describe the social system developed in the Soviet Union after the 1917 Revolution, with "atheistic" and "totalitarian" as the two adjectives most frequently used to describe that system in the Cold War mentality that has dominated opinion in the noncommunist world since World War II. Some will add "scientific" — a word that confirms for them the impression of a monolithic and unchanging system. A similar sense of immutability, demanded by revealed principles, is projected by Roman Catholicism and — to a lesser extent — the major Protestant denominations. It would seem, in consequence, that Christianity and the many theories of social organization popularly described as communist, long in conflict, are doomed so to continue forever. If, nevertheless, we look at the history of the terms "socialism" and "communism," and at the social structures that in the course of the centuries have attempted to represent their meaning, the conclusion quickly becomes debatable.

The Forerunners

"Communism" is in fact a word that describes a thousand little-related ideas and systems. It would appropriately describe the worldview of a twelfth-century Italian monk from Calabria, Joachim di Fiore, the earliest known utopian. Member of a well-connected family at the Sicilian court, Joachim became a hermit,

1

then an itinerant preacher, and finally a Benedictine monk. He interpreted the human experience as an ongoing process that would reach its culmination and perfection within human history, not in some posthistorical eschaton. Starting from the Trinitarian doctrine that is a central feature of all Christian belief, he divided the history of salvation into three epochs. The first, linked to God the Father, lasted from Adam to Christ. The second, linked to God the Son, still continued. It would, however, be soon superseded by the era of God the Spirit, more perfect than all that had gone before, a new earth without employers, without property, without a state, without rich or poor, without worship or priests. In the first, the people of God were under the Law and "were not able to attain the freedom of the Spirit.... The second status was under the Gospel and remains until the present with freedom in comparison to the past but not with freedom in comparison to the future."[1]

Joachim's apocalyptic vision has had an impact on many later thinkers. Those who identified him as one of the forerunners of modern searches for more human social structures included Friedrich Engels (1820–1895), the closest collaborator of Karl Marx (1818–1883) in his theoretical research and his revolutionary activism.[2] Jesuit theologian Henri de Lubac saw the Calabrian monk as spiritual father of Hegel and Marx.[3]

The *ejido* system of communal ownership and use of their land by Mexico's Indians and the similar property and work systems of the Andean Incas were communist. So were the Jesuit *reducciones* of Paraguay and the life of the Christian monastery, not to mention the vision of Plato's *Republic*, St. Thomas More's *Utopia*, the medieval Cathari and Albigenses, and the Anabaptists who brought Luther's ire down on them in the Peasant War. Communist also, as Marx stresses more than once, were the early Christians whose lifestyle is described in the Acts of the Apostles. "The faithful all lived together and owned everything in common; they sold their goods and possessions and shared out the proceeds among themselves according to what each one needed" (Acts 2:44–45).

Although this practice of some early Christians never became generalized, the emphasis on community of goods long continued. Harsh condemnations of private accumulation of wealth abound in the writing of the Fathers of the Church who flourished from the late second to the mid-fifth century. A passage from John Chrysostom (c. 347–407), bishop of Constantinople, reads: "For 'mine' and 'thine' — those chilly words which introduce innumerable wars into the world — should be eliminated from that holy church. . . . All things would be in common." Augustine of Hippo (354–430) agrees: "Those who wish to make room for the Lord must find pleasure not in private, but in common property."[4] Although frowned upon by the institutional church in later times, the longing for a communist lifestyle surfaced time and again in later centuries. One medieval sect that rejected private ownership called itself the *Comunati*. Another, called *Apostolici*, which committed itself to live as the Apostles of Jesus had lived and which survived into the thirteenth century, was the subject of commentary by St. Thomas Aquinas.[5]

The word "socialism" was first used in England in November 1827 in *The Cooperative Magazine* to identify the disciples of Robert Owen, pioneer of the cooperative movement; it was used in France in 1831 in *Le Semeur* and a second time the following year in *Le Globe*[6] for the followers of Saint-Simon. The term was long employed interchangeably with "communism." If any distinction was made, it was to describe as socialists those who insisted that a strong state should not only control but own all means of production, while communists were those who would abolish all private property except immediate personal goods.

Communism, as it is known today, derives principally from Karl Marx and Friedrich Engels. Both were born in Prussia, Marx the second of seven children, Engels the eldest of eight. Marx's lawyer father was Jewish but he was baptized into the Lutheran church with all his family, apparently for political rather than for religious reasons. Engels, a member of an old German Lutheran family, taught himself several languages and wrote on religion, philosophy, and politics for various German publications while working in his father's textile mill. Marx graduated with a doctorate in philosophy from Berlin University. They met in Cologne in 1842 when Marx was editor of the *Rheinische Zeitung*. After the newspaper was suppressed in 1843 because of Marx's inflammatory editorials, they went together into exile in Switzerland, Paris, Brussels, and finally England, where Engels became manager and part-owner of his father's textile mill in Manchester. Financially supported by Engels, Marx began the research at the British Museum that resulted in his most famous work, *Capital*.

Marx and Engels described their *Manifesto* of 1848 as communist rather than socialist for reasons given by Engels in his preface to the 1881 edition.

By Socialists, in 1847, were understood, on the one hand, the adherents of the various Utopian systems: Owenites in England, Fourierists in France, both of them already reduced to the position of mere sects, and gradually dying out; on the other hand, the most multifarious social quacks, who, by all manners of tinkering, professed to redress, without any danger to capital and profit, all sorts of grievances; in both cases men outside the working-class movement, and looking rather to the 'educated' classes for support. Whatever portion of the working class had become convinced of the insufficiency of mere political revolutions, and had proclaimed the necessity of a total social change, that portion then called itself Communist.... Thus Socialism was, in 1847, a middle-class movement, Communism, a working-class movement.[7]

Enlightenment and Revolution

Marx and Engels were not, however, the first to express concern about the deterioration of the conditions of the workers and their families in the Europe of their time and to propose radical, even revolutionary, social change as a remedy. Already a century before them in England and France, the two countries in which capitalism was then significantly developed, various movements had arisen. Many of these drew their inspiration from Christian sources, the Luddites in England, Wilhelm Weitling in Central Europe. Robert Owen, although personally hostile to Christianity, was for many an intellectual guide. But the Christian-inspired initiatives were never more than marginal. The church leadership always remained closely identified with governments and ruling classes. The more dynamic socialist movements, those that were to determine the quality of the ultimate challenge to capitalism, were dominated by antireligious sentiments and attitudes.

Objective grounds for this conflict existed. In France, the home of the Enlightenment, church and state formed an indistinguishable unity. Cardinals Richelieu and Mazarin were in turn the chief ministers of the monarch, brilliant men whose power was used to advance the royal prerogatives while at the same time manipulating the church to serve primarily secular ends. But the absolute monarchy which they consolidated in France and which they used religion to legitimate was diametrically opposed to everything sacred to the Enlightenment.

The dominant conviction of that extraordinary scientific, philosophical, religious, and political movement of eighteenth century Europe was that right reasoning could find true knowledge and lead society to happiness. For it, rigorous mathematical reasoning offered the means, independent of any divine revelation, to establish truth. Building on the scientific method derived from Galileo and Newton, it attacked religion because matters of faith by definition could not be subjected to scientific critique, the task made easier because much of what it attacked in contemporary religious practice richly deserved criticism: an excessive love for the miraculous and the bizarre, the Jansenistic view of God as a hard master, bitter rivalries between religious groups, use of religion to justify privilege, and failure of the powerful and wealthy believers to care for the poor and oppressed.

Christianity's first weapons of self-defense were the traditional ones of dogmatic assertion of its truths and the utilization of state sanctions to enforce its decrees. Not surprisingly, this repressive response intensified the conviction of the devotees of science that religion had to be eliminated before the new society they advocated could come into being.

What that society should be was a matter of intense debate, but its general thrust was established by the scientific experience of the period. A long history of extensive state intervention in economic matters and a recent history of middle-class dissatisfaction at being excluded from a voice in political life furnished the background. The solution, it was argued, would be found in a harmony of interests brought about by right reasoning under the stimulus of free competition, and this required the ending of the church-state alliance and the abolition both of hereditary monarchical rule and of the privileged class of nobles.

Voltaire and the Encyclopedists, men who sincerely sought to free society from dogmatism and superstition, were convinced that both church and state had to be overthrown to achieve their ends. The commercial and industrial sectors committed to the development of capitalism equally required enormous social change from the preceding mercantilist society. To implement the productive potential inherent in the capitalist mode of thinking demanded an open and enquiring society in which first the physical and later also the social sciences would flourish. Abolition of the "divine right" of kings, a system that was legitimated and buttressed by the churches, was a necessary precondition for such change. The interests of emerging capitalism thus converged with the convictions of the philosophers of the Enlightenment who saw feudal relations and absolute monarchy as unassailable unless their religious supports were first stripped away. "The Christian religion runs counter to the political health and well-being of nations," wrote Baron d'Holbach in a typical broadside. "Religion is the art of making men drunk in ecstasy in order to divert their attention from the evils heaped upon them here below by those who govern them."[8]

The Capitalist Manifesto

With the French Revolution, the old order seemed to have been utterly swept away. And, in historical retrospect, it was in fact mortally wounded. A new concept of human society and human possibilities had taken root and would inevitably sprout and blossom. But the change did not come easily or automatically. After the fall of Napoleon, the princes of Europe decided at the Congress of Vienna in 1815 to restore the "legitimate" order as it had existed before 1789. Russia, Austria, and Prussia there signed a Holy Alliance, a treaty that set out the political and ideological positions that would guide the major European powers for half a century. "Around this core were grouped the feudal dynasties of Germany, Italy and Spain, with powerful allies in all European countries, above all the Catholic church, the conservative property-owning bourgeoisie of England, and the financial aristocracy which had come to power in France after the July revolution of 1830."[9]

The basic concept of the Holy Alliance was the interdependence of religion, authority, and the divine right of kings within a framework of a paternalistic understanding of politics and the principle of solidarity among monarchs in defense of the status quo.

After an introduction in which the monarchs commit themselves to found their reciprocal relations on "the sublime truths which the eternal religion of God the Savior teaches," the treaty stipulates:

In conformity with the words of sacred scripture which command all men to look on each other as brothers, the three contracting monarchs will remain united with bonds of true and indissoluble brotherhood, and considering each other to be compatriots, on every occasion and in every place they will give each other assistance, aid, and help in time of need; and viewing themselves in relation to their subjects and their armies as fathers of families, they will guide them in the same spirit of brotherhood which inspires them to protect religion, peace, and justice.... Their majesties therefore recommend to their peoples with the most tender concern, as the only possible means to enjoy that peace that comes from a good conscience and which alone is lasting, to strengthen themselves more and more each day in the principles and in the exercise of the duties which the Divine Savior has taught to men.[10]

Britain did not openly join the Holy Alliance, because — as foreign secretary Castlereagh explained — its monarch could not recognize principles contrary to those that legitimated his rule. The Hanover dynasty's claim to the throne rested on the deposition of the Stuarts by the British Parliament and the substitution of William of Orange as king in the 1690s; and the exiled Stuart "pretenders" had not relinquished their royal claims. But Britain was a faithful if non-card-carrying member of the Alliance.

The first action of the Alliance was to reinstate the royal families dethroned by the French Revolution. They included the pope who was seen by Europe's Catholic, Protestant, and Orthodox monarchs as a powerful ally against republicanism and other heresies. The idea of democracy had, however, spread widely from France throughout Europe, and the Alliance had to intervene repeatedly, often with major military involvement and much bloodshed, to block the pressures of the people for a voice in their destiny.

Thanks to the political genius of Prince Metternich, Austria's minister of foreign affairs, the Congress of Vienna produced a coalition of nations that functioned as a counterrevolutionary "International" committed to the task of saving Europe from democracy. This Alliance forced the German Bundestag in 1819 to pass the Karlsbad Act, which suppressed in the German states freedom of thought, publication, and teaching, and which explicitly authorized armed intervention in other countries to protect absolutist forms of government. But principles did not prevent Britain from supporting the Alliance. While officially protesting the Karlsbad Act, Castlereagh congratulated Metternich in a confidential letter on his success. Similarly, the Duke of Wellington, as British prime minister, publicly protested armed intervention in Spain while privately expressing approval.

At the Treaty of Paris in November 1815, Castlereagh joined with the signatories of the Holy Alliance in the Quadruple Alliance, a structure given specific peace-keeping functions. Expanded in 1818 to include France, it was committed to maintenance of the status quo in all Europe. It did, in fact, intervene militarily on many occasions. In Spain, for example, in 1823 following a joint ultimatum signed by Russia, Austria, Prussia, and France, an army one hundred thousand strong invaded and restored an absolutist regime which immediately proceeded to slaughter all who were identified as promoting democracy. The principle of legitimacy was carried to the extreme of supporting the Sultan of Turkey who massacred tens of thousands of his Christian subjects between 1821 and 1827 while suppressing revolts in Greece. It was unimportant, Metternich said, if three or four hundred thousand people were hanged, slaughtered, or cut to pieces on the other side of Austria's eastern border. What was important was that all revolutions should be quelled. For Metternich, a Greek defeat by the Turks "appeared a matter of comparative unimportance, which might be allowed to burn itself out 'beyond the pale of civilization.' "[11]

Under the able guidance of Metternich, the Holy Alliance used religion as a means of control of all liberal movements. The pope was not a member of these groupings, but he had a voice in their deliberations. He had been represented at the Congress of Vienna by his secretary of state, Cardinal Ercole Consalvi, a skilled diplomat. While keeping a low public profile, Consalvi was indefatigable behind the scenes. "Yesterday I spent a very large part of the day," he wrote in notes dated from December 1814 to January 1815, "between the Prince von Hardenburg, the Count de Nessel-rode, and Lord Castlereagh. I came out deeply saddened from the long exchange, in the course of which we listed and discussed all the questions on the agenda." He warned them, Consalvi wrote, of the danger that resulted from changing rulers, laws, customs, and usages every half century. "Laws are a bit to which man's mouth should gradually become accustomed. The yoke of a cheerful obe-dience should be transmitted in families from one generation to the next as a memory of fatherly protection rather than as a mark of subjection." To apply the principle to the concrete situation, Con-salvi argued, meant that it was essential to rebuild solidly on the old foundation, because "the principles of the French Revolution were destructive of all order."

Consalvi noted that the Prince of Hardenburg "is as fearful of the future as I am. . . . He would build a dam against the tor-rent of wicked doctrines and impious declarations." Consalvi was concerned, however, that the restored French monarchy and the English authorities were insufficiently alert to the danger of ideas. "Several times I told Louis XVIII and the English prince regent that press freedom as established in France by royal decree is the most dangerous weapon ever placed in the hands of the adversaries of religion and the monarchy. . . . It is an injection that produces in the people an endless and restless fever."[12]

Consalvi not only recovered most of the territory that had formed the papal states before the French Revolution, but also won significant concessions for the church in all of Europe. The various monarchs ceased to press their earlier claims to keep tight control on the church in their kingdoms, seeking instead an alliance that would allow more space for ecclesiastical organizations. The si-multaneous development of the Romantic Movement in Europe provided a more sympathetic climate for traditionalist religious attitudes, although the former anticlericalism survived in certain sectors.[13]

Protestantism was the established religion in two of Europe's most important countries, Britain and Germany, as was Ortho-doxy in Russia. In all three countries the state had a controlling voice in naming the top leadership, and its subsidization of the churches further ensured their defense of its interests. Given this context, it is understandable that Protestantism and Orthodoxy should become as fully incorporated as Roman Catholicism into the counterrevolutionary International. Not surprisingly, as movements for democracy and national independence developed, they identified all three Christian religions and the secular powers as equally their enemies and they saw the need to create their own International in order to achieve their objectives. The development of such international solidarity became evident in 1848, the year in which its objectives were spelled out by Marx and Engels in *The Communist Manifesto*.[14] In May of that year, workers in Paris stormed the Chamber of Deputies to demand war against Russia in support of the Polish revolution. Five months later, Vienna's workers took to the barricades to prevent dispatch of troops to crush rebellion in Hungary.[15] The workers of the world had begun to unite.

Chapter 2

The Catholic Response

Revolt was in the air all over Europe in 1848, and the papacy was not exempted. Riots in Rome forced Pope Pius IX to flee to Gaeta. Three years earlier, when he was elected pope and took charge of the government of the Papal States, he had sought to appease the progressives by granting a constitution. Simultaneously, however, he issued an encyclical letter, *Qui Pluribus* (1846), in which he denounced the prevailing dangers to religion. They included the Carbonari and other secret societies, "the crafty Bible Societies which renew the old skills of the heretics and ceaselessly force on people of all kinds, even the uneducated, gifts of the Bible," and people who claimed that all religions were basically the same. The Carbonari were particularly pernicious because their objective was to unite Italy, and that would mean an end to the temporal power of the papacy. For the first time, Pius listed among the enemies of the church "the unspeakable doctrine of communism, as it is called, a doctrine most opposed to the very natural law." If accepted, he warned, "the complete destruction of everyone's laws, government, property, and even of human society itself would follow."[1]

Pius IX (1846–1878)
The reference to communism is a passing one, and no attempt is made to define exactly what it comprises. Neither does Pius IX get down to specifics in the two condemnations of communism

that followed his flight to Gaeta. One is in an 1849 allocution, *Quibus Quantisque*,[2] that deals with the situation in Rome. "Who does not know that Rome...has now become the lair of roaring beasts, since it is full of men from all nations, including apostates, heretics, teachers of communism, as it is called, or of socialism, and all of them fired with a burning hatred of Catholic truth?" In the same year, while still in Gaeta, he returned to the subject in the encyclical, *Nostis et Nobiscum* (1849). Having denounced "their impious teaching and the plague of their novel theories," Pius declared that

it is now generally known that the special goal of their proponents is to introduce to the people the pernicious fictions of socialism and communism by misapplying the terms "liberty" and "equality." The final goal shared by these teachings, whether of communism or socialism, even if approached differently, is to excite by continuous disturbance workers and others, especially those of the lower class, whom they have deceived by their lies and deluded by the promise of a happier condition. They are preparing them for plundering, stealing, and usurping, first the Church's and then everyone's property. After this they will profane all law, human and divine, to destroy divine worship and to subvert the entire ordering of civil societies.[3]

Instead of listening to such people, the pope advised, the poor should resign themselves to their fate.

Warn your faithful that the nature of human society obligates its members to obey its lawfully established authorities.... Let the poor and all the wretched recall their great debt to the Catholic religion which keeps the teaching of Christ unspoiled and preaches it publicly. For he proclaimed that whatever benefits are conferred on the poor and wretched are likewise conferred on himself. Furthermore, he wishes that all be informed of the special account he will take of these works of mercy on the Day of Judgment.... This proclamation of Christ and his other stern warnings on the use of wealth and its dangers have meant that the condition of the poor and wretched in Catholic nations is much less harsh than in any other nations.... Let our poor recall the teaching of Christ himself that they should not be sad in their condition, since their very poverty makes lighter their journey to salvation, provided that they bear their need with patience and are poor not alone in possessions, but in spirit too.... All the faithful should know too that the old kings of the pagan nations and other chiefs of state misused their power in more serious ways and more often. The faithful should reckon it to the credit of our most holy religion that princes in Christian times feared the stern judgment in store for governors and the eternal punishment prepared for sinners, in which the strong will suffer strong torments. Because of this fear, they have ruled the peoples subject to them more justly and clemently.[4]

If we look at the situation of Europe in 1849, the papal analysis of the motives of the promoters of unrest among the workers and of the results of their efforts makes considerable sense, as does the advice to suffer the apparently inevitable with patience. Revolutions had rocked all Europe the previous year, with attacks on rulers, assassinations of ministers, sieges of legislative assemblies. In these struggles, the socialist and communist groups, who at that time were still minorities, joined forces with the middle classes and called the workers to man the barricades. And just as in France in the 1790s, the workers were the ones who were slaughtered but the beneficiaries were the middle classes. The liberal constitutional regimes established in several countries were no more sympathetic to the proletariat than the absolute monarchs had been. When Pius appealed to the Catholic powers, France, Austria, Naples, and Spain, to intervene militarily, French troops quickly liquidated the Roman Republic and restored the Inquisition, censorship of the press, and government by monsignori who answered only to themselves.

The short-term judgment was not unreasonable. It is, nevertheless, difficult to forgive Pius and his advisers for their failure to read and respond to the signs of the times, or their inability to see any motivation other than "a hatred of religion" in those who at extreme personal risk advocated social change. Rome's worldwide contacts provided access to unequalled sources of information. The Jesuit monthly review *Civiltà Cattolica* was founded in 1850 under the pope's patronage, and within six months it had twelve thousand subscribers in Italy and abroad. Its pages during its first quarter century provide extensive discussion of socialism and communism and analysis of the economic, social, political, moral, philosophical, and historical factors that favored the spread

of ideas advocating radical social change. Although church administration was less centralized than it became during the following
century, the Holy See had constant reports from every part of the
world. Yet one man of this time, dependent on a friend's subsidization to survive, has left us in *Capital* a description of the
contemporary human condition that is totally absent from the
papal evaluations, a description that is both meticulously docu-
mented and permeated with concern for and commitment to the
victims of injustice.

The picture was not a pretty one. In England, home of capitalism, women and eight-year-old children worked twelve and more
hours a day, being rewarded — as demanded by the natural law of
supply and demand — with what was essential to support life and
thus ensure smooth and uninterrupted production. In Ireland, a
million starved to death while wheat sufficient to feed all of them
was exported. The peasants were being evicted from Scotland's
Highlands to make room for grouse ranches. In the United States,
Native Americans were being cheated and tricked and killed in
the name of progress. It was the heyday of the robber barons
who perfected the techniques that had despoiled Britain's masses.
Australia's natives, the country's owners by all equity, were being
fed the poisoned carcasses of sheep. And the power brokers of
Christian Europe were dividing the helpless body of Africa into
bits and pieces with total disregard of the wishes and cultures of
the inhabitants.

Clinging pathetically to the defunct era of absolute monarchy, the crumbling ramparts manned with theological fulminations, Pius IX continued to the end to reject the notion that all
human beings are entitled by right to a voice in their destiny.
The message of *Nostis et Nobiscum* is repeated in the encyclicals, *Quanto Conficiamur Maerore* (1863) and *Quanta Cura* (1864),
as well as in the Syllabus of Errors appended to *Quanta Cura*.
Ironically, the main thrust of these documents was to refute the
principles of liberty and equality professed by the French Revolution, the principles undergirding the bourgeois society which
the socialists challenged. There is only a passing reference (in
the Syllabus) to "socialism, communism, secret societies, Bible societies, clerical-liberal societies," with the comment that "pests

of this description have been frequently rebuked in the severest terms."[5]

Toward the end of his pontificate, Pius IX seems to have become more aware of the seriousness of the challenge of the First International — which Marx had founded in 1864 — to his concept of society. In late 1871, several French newspapers charged the International with having set fire to Paris, and newspapers in the United States claimed that the Chicago fire of October 1871 was similarly the work of the International.[6] As various European governments were discussing the appropriate action to be taken against the International, Adolphe Thiers, named chief executive of France by the National Assembly in February 1871 and elected President of the Republic six months later, recommended that its members should be treated as the Spanish Inquisition had treated heretics. When Thiers was challenged on the grounds that the right of political asylum was based on Christian teaching, Pius supported Thiers. Speaking to a deputation of Swiss Catholics, he said:

Your government, which is republican, feels obliged to make great sacrifices in the interests of so-called freedom. It grants asylum to characters of the worst kind.... These gentlemen of the International are to be feared because they labor in the cause of the eternal enemy of God and mankind. What is to be gained, then, in affording them protection?[7]

Leo XIII (1878–1903)

Pope Leo XIII, who succeeded Pius IX in 1878, shared his predecessor's evaluation of the contemporary world but differed from him in his approach to it. Recognizing that liberal capitalism had replaced absolutism as the dominant political system of government, he decided it was his duty to find ways to live with it. On the day of his election he wrote to the rulers of Russia, Germany, and Switzerland, in all of which Catholics were subject to legal discriminations. Having notified them in friendly language of his election, he asked them to grant freedom of conscience to their Catholic subjects and promised in return the fidelity and submission of Catholics to the political power.

The official responses to this initiative were reserved. But an opening had been made and results followed. Before the end of the year, Prince Otto von Bismarck, first chancellor of the German Empire, had begun negotiations with the papal nuncio to Munich. Some of the Kulturkampf laws against the Catholic church were soon relaxed. Diplomatic relations were renewed in 1884 and a modus vivendi reached in 1887. When Alexander III came to the throne in Russia in 1883, an agreement was reached under which a few Catholic dioceses were authorized and some of the laws restricting the clergy were modified.[8]

Four years later Leo took an even more daring step, one that would have far-reaching consequences. He told French Catholics to stop dreaming about a restoration of bygone monarchies and instead to work constructively to support and improve the Republic. Not only had French Catholics not accepted the French Revolution, but they had never made peace with the secular, liberal regimes that followed the downfall of Napoleon. This struggle between church and state continued to split France for a century after the French Revolution. In the revolutions of 1789, 1830, 1848, and 1871, the influence of the church was under attack, and the Paris Commune formally separated church and state. But in each period of counterrevolution the church regained, and at times increased, its strength. For the most part it supported the Second Empire which resulted from Louis Napoleon's coup d'état in December 1851. When the Third Republic replaced the Second Empire on its collapse in 1870 following French defeat in the Franco-Prussian War, Catholics and monarchists formed a majority in the National Assembly for six years, and the Catholics won significant benefits, including a law that allowed them to open their own universities. In 1876, however, an anticlerical government came to power and in 1880 it dissolved most religious orders and enacted laws designed to limit Catholic activities.

Such was the conflictual relationship between church and state in France when Leo decided to intervene. The response of the French Catholics to the papal overture was, however, absolutely negative. Leo nevertheless insisted, finally setting out his reasoning in an encyclical letter, *Au Milieu des Sollicitudes* (1892). France, he noted, had over the previous century had several forms of government, the Empire, the Monarchy, and the Republic, each of which had positive qualities to commend it. He then laid down the rather extraordinary principle that "all citizens are bound to accept these governments and not attempt their overthrow or a change in their form."[9]

However, he continued, people don't choose their forms of government in an orderly, academic debate. They do so by a continuous process of trial and error. Nor are they so virtuous as always to change their forms of government according to the rules of justice. They often use force. Then what should be our response when this happens?

In the wake of violent crises, too often of a bloody character, . . . pre-existing governments totally disappear. . . . From that time forward a social need obtrudes itself upon the nation: it must provide for itself without delay. . . . This social need justifies the creation and the existence of new governments, whatever form they take. . . . Consequently, when new governments representing this immutable power are constituted, their acceptance is not only permissible but even obligatory, being imposed by the need of the social good.[10]

This, Leo concluded, is what has happened in France. In consequence, even though the new government was sectarian and harassed Catholics in many ways, they should accept its legitimacy and work constructively within its framework to eliminate its defects.

In fact, the French Catholics ignored Leo, and the Republic long continued to enforce and increase its antichurch measures. In addition, Leo acted inconsistently in refusing to apply the same principle to Italy, where the church-state conflict was not resolved until Pius XI signed a Concordat with Mussolini in 1928. But the principle asserted in *Au Milieu des Sollicitudes* became and has continued to this time to be the guiding principle of papal policy on social change, even if today it would be phrased with more nuances. Accept the established regime; do nothing to destroy it or change its form.

The formula does not automatically solve every concrete issue. But it marks a historic change in the Holy See's stand vis-à-vis civil society. Until that time, its fulminations had for a century been directed principally against liberalism and rationalism, the ideological foundations of capitalism. Condemnation of socialism, communism, and anarchism had become more frequent since mid-century, but these movements had remained peripheral in papal thought. Liberalism and rationalism were judged to be the powerful enemies, the ones that had to be overcome if religion was to survive. Now we have a re-evaluation of the situation, a decision that the most serious threat to religion comes from the socialist and communist movements, and that it is possible to make working agreements with triumphant liberalism. While the theoretical criticisms of liberalism and rationalism remain in place, in practice the derived political systems are not only recognized but supported; the church's anathemas are instead turned against the more radical sociopolitical reformers who would use, to the extent necessary, the same violent means to achieve their ends as had been used to substitute absolute monarchy with liberal democracy.

Roman Catholic membership was strongest in the countries of Western Europe that declined as capitalism throve, and its membership in prosperous capitalist countries was strongest among the propertyless wage-earners ruthlessly exploited by the robber barons of the nineteenth century. Not only its professed principles but its pragmatic self-interest would logically have placed it on the side of these countries and social groups exploited by capitalism. Instead, an obsession with protecting the temporal power of the papacy and a long history of subservience to the rich and powerful impelled the Roman church to devote its energies and its scholastically-honed ingenuity to a philosophical defense of the system under which its members groaned. The theses were developed in a long series of papal documents and presented as expressions of an objective and unchanging natural order. While ignored by the statesmen and captains of industry to whom they were addressed, they gradually became the common currency of capitalism's propagandists, by whom even today they continue to be used. But the error did have a tragic result. It played a significant part in the alienation from the church of the working classes of Europe.

Marxism has long been singled out by the defenders of capitalism as the enemy. In the 1890s, however, it was not yet seen as the focal point of the radical movements. Utopian socialism had not survived the failure of the revolutionary outbreaks of 1848, and the foundation of the First International in London in 1864 was an attempt to weld together a heterogeneous collection of left-wing theoreticians and activists. It is true that Marx was the central figure in this organization and the one with the most highly structured body of thought as expressed already in *The Communist Manifesto* and later more fully in *Capital*. It was not he, however, but the anarchist Bakunin who attracted Leo's attention, in part because the radical movement in Italy — and also in Catholic Spain — was predominantly anarchist, but also in part because in the second half of the nineteenth century Bakunin had a wide following in all of Europe. Such was the appeal of his doctrine of the abolition of the state, that in 1872, to prevent Bakunin from getting control of the First International, Marx moved its headquarters to the United States where it languished and soon died.

It was the anarchists that Leo had primarily in mind when he wrote *Quod Apostolici Muneris* (1878).

We speak of that sect of men who, under various and almost barbaric names, are called socialists, communists, or nihilists, and who, spread over all the world, and bound together by the closest ties in a wicked confederacy, no longer seek the shelter of secret meetings, but openly and boldly marching in the light of day, strive to bring to a head what they have long been planning — the overthrow of all civil society whatsoever.... The revered majesty and power of kings have won such fierce hatred from their seditious people that disloyal traitors, impatient of all restraint, have more than once within a short period raised their arms in impious attempt against the lives of their own sovereigns.... They refuse obedience to the higher powers to whom, according to the admonition of the apostle, every soul ought to be subject, and who derive the right of governing from God; and they proclaim the absolute equality of all men in rights and duties. They debase the natural union of man and woman, which is held sacred even among barbarous peoples; and its bond, by which the family is chiefly held together, they weaken or even deliver up to lust. Lured in fine by the greed of present goods, which is the root of all evils,... they assail the right of property sanctioned by natural law; and by a scheme of horrible wickedness, while they seem desirous of caring for the needs and satisfying the desires of all men, they strive to seize and hold in common whatever has been acquired either by title of lawful inheritance, or by labor of brains and hands, or by thrift in one's mode of life.[11]

This description of the enemy follows closely the program of the Alliance of Socialist Democracy founded by Bakunin when he broke with Marx. The primary emphasis on Bakuninism in *Quod Apostolici Muneris* does not, however, mean that reference to Marxism was entirely absent. One of the first French Marxists, Jules Guesde, quickly wrote a commentary on the encyclical in which he insisted that it had accurately described his program, a social revolution challenging all the things Christians stand for, a world from which God is disappearing so that only free men will remain to carry on the struggle.[12] And in *Rerum Novarum* (1891), the concern with Marxism has grown. In this encyclical, for the first time, Rome moves beyond condemnations to attempt to formulate a coherent alternative doctrine.

The two issues that are explicitly faced are the Marxist rejection of private property and its theory of class struggle.[13] The former would upset society, enslave the citizens, eliminate economic stimuli, contradict the natural rights of the individual, and end by organizing equality into destitution. The latter wrongly represents classes as natural enemies, whereas "capital cannot do without labor, nor labor without capital." Although the Marxist claim that the wage system is inherently unjust and the correlative theory of surplus value are not explicitly attacked, the underlying premise of the encyclical is that the wage system is inherently legitimate. All that is needed is to keep profit within "just limits." What this did was to commit the church to support the capitalist system on the ground that it needed only to be reformed, not to be radically transformed. We have here the beginning of the developmentalism that continues to be the position of conservative Christians, and of the Vatican, though increasingly challenged by the theology of liberation.

Pius XI (1922–1939)

Developmentalism means taking an essentially anti-Marxist stand, an option for capitalism. While rejecting socialism, however, it has incorporated socialist elements from the outset, over the years steadily adding more. A major step was *Quadragesimo Anno* (1931), Pius XI's encyclical on the fortieth anniversary of *Rerum Novarum*. Much had happened in the interval. The virtuous Christian employers on whom *Rerum Novarum* had relied to improve the lot of the worker had failed to materialize. Socialism, in consequence, had won the allegiance of a steadily growing number of the world's dispossessed, especially after the October Revolution (1917) provided it with a power base in Russia. Big business between the two world wars adapted to the economic pressure for "venture" capital, transforming liberal capitalism — made up of many small firms — into monopolistic concentrations that constituted a true capitalist regime and that, in 1929, plunged the world into a deeper economic crisis than it had ever previously known. In response to the crisis of capitalism, Germany and Italy had adopted corporatism as the official socio-economic system, an experience in which they were followed by Hungary, Spain, and Portugal.

Socialism had also changed in two important aspects. A regime had been solidly established in Russia that not only proclaimed itself Marxist but presented itself as guardian and exclusive orthodox interpreter of an all-encompassing worldview. In addition, in 1921, the socialist movement had split into revolutionaries and reformers, supporters respectively of an abrupt passage to socialism and of a smooth and democratic evolution that would be the logical result of capitalism's own contradictions. This split finally resolved the semantic problem. Communism would thenceforth mean the revolutionary model; socialism, the evolutionary.

Pius XI seized on the distinction to introduce important changes in the church's social teaching, in effect identifying and accepting several elements in the Marxist criticism of capitalism as legitimate. He agreed with Lenin that "free enterprise" must evolve into monopoly capitalism, "an international imperialism whose country is where profit is," a system not able to curb or control itself, or to direct economic life, and in consequence ultimately self-destructive. The free market, Pius charged, "of its own nature" concentrates power in anti-social types, in those "who fight most violently and give least heed to their conscience." It is Darwinism gone mad.

As for socialism, while both kinds were to be condemned because of their "opposition to the Christian faith," the violent form, Pius declared, was obviously worse than the other. He singled out as one of the most objectionable elements of communism its commitment to "merciless class warfare." It is not at all clear that this description does justice to Marx's thought. In his view, social antagonisms result from necessary change and must exist until the historical process has led to the disappearance of one of the classes in this conflict. He also insisted, however, on the active role played by the human agent in every historical process. Lenin stressed that aspect and consequently urged revolutionaries to make the class conflict more bitter in order to speed the process of solution. That Pius should condemn unnecessary or irresponsible violence is logical. His blanket condemnation of class conflict, however, goes much further. The traditional Catholic position on the right of people to overthrow a tyrant would seem to envisage circumstances in which class conflict would be a legitimate element of defense against institutionalized violence.

One unhappy carryover from the mindset of Pius IX was reasserted in *Quadragesimo Anno*, the notion of a fixed order determined by God and not to be challenged by humans. The workers, Pius XI wrote, "will accept without rancour the place which divine providence has assigned to them." It was a position that had been spelled out in more detail by his predecessor, Pius X: "Human society as established by God is made up of unequal elements.... Accordingly, it is in conformity with the order of human society as established by God that there be rulers and ruled, employers and employees, learned and ignorant, nobles and plebeians."[14] It would be expressed once again by Pius XI in a letter to the bishops of the United States, *Sertum Letitiae* (1939). "The history of every age," Pius wrote, "teaches that there were always rich and poor; that it will always be so we may gather from the unchanging tenor of human destinies."[15] Subsequent papal documents, however, have ceased to stress that particular claim.

To sum up, Pius XI in *Quadragesimo Anno* offered a more constructive and detailed evaluation of socialism than his predecessors, distinguishing two kinds. The more violent form "has sunk into communism" and seeks "unrelenting class warfare and absolute extermination of private ownership." The other "professes the rejection of violence" and modifies "the class struggle and the abolition of private property." Triumphally, and with scant regard for the reality of history, Pius suggested that this socialism "inclines toward and in a certain sense approaches the truth which Christian tradition has always held sacred," formulating programs that "at times come very near those that Christian reformers of society justly insist upon."[16]

The encyclical noted three specific points of approach: (1) a recognition that violence is not always necessary for social reform; (2) a withdrawal from the class struggle in favor of dialogue to bring the classes into harmony; (3) a narrowing of the attack on private property, a call to eliminate abuses rather than destroy the institution itself. Nevertheless, for Pius, the errors of communism still predominate: our true end is rejected in favor of material well-being; the individual is subordinated totally to society; no firm foundation for authority remains; the "socialist man" is committed to values incompatible with those of Christianity.

In consequence, Pius concluded, Christians may work within their own organizations to promote the positive elements in the socialist program, but they must not join socialist organizations. "Whether considered as a doctrine, or a historical fact, or a movement," socialism "cannot be reconciled with the teaching of the Catholic church, because its concept of society itself is utterly foreign to Christian truth."[17]

A previously overlooked indictment of communism — soon to achieve pride of place in Pius XI's encyclical *Divini Redemptoris* (1937) — emerges in *Quadragesimo Anno*: its preaching and practice of militant atheism. The encyclical concentrated its attacks on the dialectical and historical materialism of which the Bolsheviks claimed to be the guardians and orthodox interpreters, and which in their interpretation would eliminate God and the whole body of Christian dogmas. Their project, Pius argued, tended to undermine the natural foundations of the human personality and the family. It would bring about the collectivization of society and enclose it in the economic sphere. In addition, it was totally utopian when it prophesied the withering away and ultimate disappearance of the state.

"The doctrine of modern communism, which is often concealed under the most seductive trappings," Pius wrote, is in substance based on the principles of dialectical and historical materialism previously advocated by Marx, of which the theoreticians of bolshevism claim to possess the only genuine interpretation. According to this doctrine there is in the world only one reality, matter, the blind forces of which evolve into plant, animal and man. Even human society is nothing but a phenomenon and form of matter, evolving in the same way. By a law of inexorable necessity and through a perpetual conflict of forces, matter moves towards the final synthesis of a classless society. In such a doctrine, as is evident, there is no room for the idea of God; there is no difference between matter and spirit, between soul and body; there is neither survival of the soul after death nor any hope in a future life. Insisting on the dialectical aspect of their materialism, the communists claim that the conflict which carries the world towards its final synthesis can be accelerated by man. Hence they endeavor to sharpen the antagonisms which arise between the various classes of society. Thus the class struggle with its consequent violent hate and destruction takes on the aspects of a crusade for the progress of humanity. On the other hand, all other forces whatever, as long as they resist such systematic violence, must be annihilated as hostile to the human race.[18]

By focusing his criticisms on Marxism as interpreted by the Bolsheviks, Pius was steadily opening more space between his position and that of his predecessors. The logic of his argument was that the more socialism moved from the Bolshevik understanding of Marx, the more acceptable it became. Pius gave no indication that this evolution ("drift") had not resulted from any effort of the Marxists to make peace with Christianity but from the internal logic of the system and the change in the historical situation caused by the concomitant evolution of capitalism.

John XXIII (1958–1963)

Pope John XXIII opened still further space with his encyclicals *Mater et Magistra* (1961) and *Pacem in Terris* (1963). He accepted the actual and objective impulse of contemporary society, which he correctly described as its intense drive to socialization, collectivization, and planetarization. He made it clear that capitalism, no less than socialism, was evolving toward a kind of collectivism, and that both the capitalist and the socialist kind of collectivism produced alienation. In his view, it might be more difficult for capitalism to

eliminate the basic injustices it nurtures than it would be for socialism to purge itself of its errors. This description reflects — and at
least implicitly approves of — the accelerating process of development of ever more complex and interrelated structures of society,
as described by Marx, Teilhard de Chardin, and other social scientists. Pope John is thus light years distant from the world of fixed
essences and the socioeconomic system immutably determined by
God in which Pius IX had lived. John criticized contemporary
neocapitalism, the lack of social progress to match the obvious
economic advances, the rapid concentration of wealth resulting
from auto-financing by industry, the failure to give workers any
real voice in economic decision-making at the national level. John
was reading the signs of the times, as the socialists had long been
doing. Marx had made the same analysis of capitalism a century
before him. Now John was saying that we had acquired a level
of control of the material world that should not be left to a few
to manipulate for private gain, that such things as nuclear energy,
genetic engineering, automation, cybernetics, conquest of space,
and instant communications were the inheritance of all so that all
should share in their control and benefits.

John took yet another giant step in *Pacem in Terris* when he
distinguished between the doctrine of communism on the one hand
and the movements or systems derived from it on the other:

False philosophical teachings regarding the nature, origin, and destiny of
the universe and of man cannot be identified with historical movements
that have economic, cultural, or political ends, not even when these movements have originated from those teachings and have drawn and still draw
inspiration therefrom.

Vatican Council II in its Constitution on the Church in the Modern World and later Pope John Paul II would further emphasize
John XXIII's insistence on the social purpose and function of property, thus bringing papal teaching on property even closer to Marx's
attitude to it as expressed in *The Communist Manifesto*. "The distinguishing feature of communism," he had written,

is not the abolition of property generally, but the abolition of bourgeois
property. But modern bourgeois private property is the final and most

complete expression of the system of producing and appropriating products that is based on class antagonism, on the exploitation of the many by the few.... You are horrified at our intending to do away with private property. But in your existing society private property is already done away with for nine tenths of the population; its existence for the few is solely due to its nonexistence in the hands of those nine tenths. You reproach us, therefore, with intending to do away with a form of property the necessary condition for whose existence is the nonexistence of any property for the immense majority of society.... Communism deprives no man of the power to appropriate the products of society; all that it does is to deprive him of the power to subjugate the labor of others by means of such appropriation.[19]

Paul VI (1963–1978)

Pope Paul VI carried the official church position closer to that of the socialists in three respects. In *Octogesima Adveniens* (1971), written to commemorate the eightieth anniversary of *Rerum Novarum*, he reaffirmed the commitment of the church to active participation in building a new world in the spirit of John XXIII and the Vatican Council. This attitude contrasts startlingly with the mindset of Pius IX — reaffirmed in the twentieth century by Pius X and Pius XI — the notion of a fixed order of society and of social roles determined by God and not to be challenged by humans. He stressed the development of a pluralism of interpretations inside Marxism and the evolution of socialist movements, with the inference that some forms might no longer fall under the earlier blanket condemnations. And he told Christians that, as social scientists, they might legitimately use the Marxist analysis of society, including the idea of class war, with appropriate safeguards against ideological errors.

John Paul II (1978–)

Pope John Paul II, the first Polish pope, is known for theological conservatism and an understandable aversion to socialism as institutionalized in the Soviet Union and its satellites. His copious output of encyclicals and other statements reveals, nevertheless, a worldview incorporating Marxist thought far more than any of his predecessors. In philosophy John Paul was deeply influenced by Emmanuel Mounier, founder of a philosophy of personalism, the belief that a person as a spiritual being maintains existence by adhering to a hierarchy of freely accepted values. Following Mounier, John Paul stresses the transcendence of the personal over the social and of Christian faith over the historical. He agrees with Marx on the centrality of work, the subject of his encyclical *Laborem Exercens*. He sees work as a "fundamental" dimension of human existence, but he does not see work — the creative act of the human — as a totalizing principle in the way Marx does. It is true that he gives his own interpretation to such Marxist terms and ideas as alienation, transformation of nature, proletarianization, social subject, and opposition between capital and labor.[20] His constant use of them, however, cannot but make Catholics more comfortable with Marxist ideas, thus contributing to the ongoing dialogue.

Chapter 3

Utopian Socialists

Programs of social change that derived from purely humanist —
and usually antireligious — worldviews were paralleled in many
countries from early in the nineteenth century by movements ap-
pealing to Christian motives for bettering the lot of the workers.
The development of a class of wage laborers in England and France,
the two countries first deeply affected by the rise of capitalism, increased significantly the number of destitute people. It also made
the destitute more visible. They were now huddled together in
industrial cities, no longer spread through the countryside. It was
understandable that the clergy and others brought into direct contact with them would search for ways to help.

England

Robert Owen (1771–1858), the founder of English socialism and
of the cooperative movement, was the operator of a textile mill in
Scotland. He established what he called "home colonies," combining industrial and agricultural cooperatives, on both sides of the
Atlantic. The most famous was located at New Harmony in Indi-
ana. He had a significant following for some thirty years, but after
about 1833 the several settlements he had established in Scotland
and in the United States to test his theories withered away. Owen
was a determinist and aggressively opposed to religion. He insisted that character was entirely the product of environment and

education, from which it would follow that a change of structures would automatically make people virtuous.

His faith in human nature would not allow him to accept the then current theological teaching that people were naturally depraved, a viewpoint that underlay his opposition to religion as an obstacle to human progress. The failure of his experimental communities would show the inadequacy of his own formula for changing society. But his emphasis on the need to change structures did have an impact that extended to those who identified themselves as Christian socialists.

A new structure that would profoundly affect society appeared in Britain in 1829, the first trade union in that country, the Grand General Union of Spinners. It was headed by John Doherty, an Irishman, who a year later founded the National Association of United Trades for the Protection of Labour.[1] Robert Owen entered the same field in 1834 with the Grand National Consolidated Trades Union, but his efforts as a labor organizer were no more successful than his cooperatives. Nearly a half century would pass before the semi-clandestine trade unions would acquire full legal status and lead to the creation of the British Labour Party.

Though in no sense himself a socialist, John Wesley (1703–1791) merits mention as one who prepared the atmosphere for what became known as Christian Socialism. Methodism was developed in England in the second half of the eighteenth century by Wesley, an Anglican clergyman, who was outraged by the failure of the established religion to concern itself about the working classes. He had long tried to reform Anglicanism from within but found himself so constrained under its control that he finally set up his own church.

A Royalist and a staunch advocate of law and order, he had a genuine sense of compassion for the poor. His direct involvement and that of his associates with poor people developed among Methodists a commitment to social justice, to the antislavery movement then gaining momentum, and to moderation in the use of material things. Before the end of the century, one of Wesley's Irish disciples, William Thompson, was promoting socialist ideas and calling for such radical changes as universal suffrage and democratic forms of government.[2]

Methodism inspired in many leaders of working class movements in England a zeal for justice, a spirit of persistence, and a biblical basis for their commitment. Wesley and other nineteenth-century evangelicals made another important, if unintended, contribution to social change by promoting literacy. To encourage more people to read the Bible, they started "Sunday Schools," which educated illiterate workers, in the process enlightening them to the evils of the world and giving them one of the tools needed in order to change it.

The first major figure in Christian Socialism was John Malcolm Forbes Ludlow (1821–1911). Born in India, he grew up in France and made a career as a lawyer in London. His education in France had given him an understanding of the meaning of democracy not shared by his English contemporaries. Monarchy for them was a divinely sanctioned guarantor of order and discipline; for him, a government "based wholly upon the interests of a family, or rather of one old man."[3]

In 1848, when the Revolution broke out in Paris, he went to see for himself. His reaction was enthusiastic. "After the gagging of the Louis Philippe regime," he recorded, "the whole city seemed to be bubbling into speech." He thereupon conceived the idea of "Christianizing socialism." It was not enough, he insisted, to help the poor to survive in their misery, as the well-intentioned around him were doing; they had to be helped out of their misery. He accordingly argued that if Christianity failed to meet this challenge, "it would be shaken to its foundations, precisely because socialism appealed to the higher and not to the lower instincts of the working class."[4]

Returning to England, he joined with John Frederick Denison Maurice (1805–1872), an Anglican clergyman, and the poet Charles Kingsley (1819–1875), to issue a call to the "Workmen of England" and to start a weekly publication called *Politics for the People*. Ludlow was its co-editor, and he also edited *The Christian Socialist*, which they started in 1851. They held that Christianity and socialism were interdependent, so that neither could survive without the other. Their socialism, however, was based rather on the New Testament than on Marxist scientific or determinist rationales.

Some of the revolutionary spirit of Paris quickly infected the English workers. They saw in the Chartist movement the vehicle to assert their rights. Actually, the Chartist demands were modest: universal adult male suffrage, a secret ballot, elimination of property qualifications that prevented worker representatives from standing for Parliament. But they were totally unacceptable to the landed and commercial aristocracy that then monopolized political power in England.

A mass demonstration was called for April 10, 1848, at Kennington Common, London, to be followed by a march to the House of Commons to present the petitions. The summons to the demonstration instructed the marchers to disperse "peaceably" afterward. But the authorities were taking no chances. They massed troops and volunteers at Kennington Common and broke up the procession before the Chartists could begin to march. The movement never recovered from the blow.

Ludlow and his friends decided to move into the vacuum and offer new political leadership to the workers. It was a role for which they were not particularly gifted. Kingsley called himself a "radical reformer," though he seemed concerned with individual rather than with social or political reform. Ludlow had more political sophistication, but his philosophy was naive, being based on "brotherhood and cooperation." His devotion to religion caused him to squelch dissent because he feared it might create schisms. Maurice was a charismatic figure, more concerned with morality than with the doctrinal content of Christianity. He preached a social revolution in opposition to the narrow moralism of contemporary Anglicanism. When the three met on the afternoon and evening of April 10, they decided to put up posters bearing a proclamation to "The Workmen of England." Its purpose was to steer the workers away from the path of violence, assuring them that they in fact had friends in high places who could be trusted to take care of their needs.

These are friends, they wrote,

who expect nothing from you but who love you, because you are their brothers, and who fear God and therefore cannot neglect you, his children, men who are drudging and sacrificing themselves to get you your rights, men who know what your rights are better than you know yourselves, who are trying to get you something nobler than charters and dozens of Acts of Parliament.... Do not mean license when you cry for liberty.... The Almighty God, and Jesus Christ, the poor man who dies for poor men, will bring freedom for you, though all the Mammonites on earth were against you.... There will be no true freedom without virtue, no true science without religion, no true industry without the fear of God and love to your fellow-citizens. Workers of England, be wise and then you *must* be free, for you will be *fit* to be free.

Not surprisingly, the Chartists seem to have completely ignored this appeal to patience and forbearance. What is more surprising is that a socialist movement of some substance finally emerged from such an unpromising start. Nor was the philosophy or prospectus of the movement formulated in the first issue of *Politics for the People* more promising:

Politics have been separated from Christianity; religious men have supposed that their only business was with the world to come; political men have declared that the present world is governed on entirely different principles from that.... *Politics for the People* cannot be separated from Religion. They must start from Atheism or from the acknowledgment that a Living and Righteous God is ruling in human society no less than in the natural world.... The world is governed by God; this is the rich man's warning; this is the poor man's comfort; this is the real hope in the consideration of all questions;... this is the pledge that Liberty, Fraternity, Unity, under some conditions or other, are intended for every people under heaven.

Given the reality described in Engels's *Condition of the Working-classes in England* and in Marx's *Capital*, it is hardly surprising that the authors of such appeals were, in Ludlow's own later admission, "distrusted or unheeded by the great bulk of the working classes." The weekly *Politics for the People* survived for only seventeen issues. But Ludlow and his associates did have an impact on some Anglican clergymen who called upon the church "to desist from its practice of threatening the workers' damnation for insubordination to their employers, demanding instead that the church use its influence to bring about an end to exploitation."[5]

The program put forth by Ludlow and his associates hardly deserves to be called socialist. During the 1850s they stressed mostly the idea of producer cooperatives based on French models. They wanted cooperation rather than collectivism or state intervention, profit sharing and copartnership rather than public ownership. Many of them favored Henry George's "single tax" as a technique for producing a more equitable society without recourse to violence. George was a popular lecturer in England, and his reputation and influence grew further with the publication in England of *Progress and Poverty*. His legal, nonrevolutionary, parliamentary device of a steadily increasing toll on the increment of land values, raised eventually to the point of virtual confiscation, won wide approval.

Increasing social pressures brought a gradual radicalization of the movement. The Guild of St. Matthew, founded in 1877 and dominated by Stewart Headlam (1847–1924), quickly developed two currents of opinion, one more specifically socialist and sympathetic to the contemporary currents of secular socialism influenced by Bakunin and Marx. The internal conflict became so acute as to cause a split in 1889, the defectors forming the more moderate Christian Social Union, a middle- and upper-middle-class group "held together by Oxford, public school, and clerical ties."[6] Five years later, the more radical element created the Christian Socialist League, which grew to six thousand members, including many Church of England bishops. It provided a platform for advocates of socialist collectivism, to include the complete nationalization of the means of production, distribution, and exchange.

The changed mood in the established church was expressed more formally in 1888 when 145 of its bishops, following the Lambeth Pan-Anglican Conference, signed a letter deploring "excessive inequality in the distribution of this world's goods, vast accumulation and desperate poverty side by side," affirmed the duty of the Christian church "to aid every wise endeavor that has for its object the material and moral welfare of the poor," and instructed the clergy in their preaching to show "how much of what is good and true in socialism is to be found in the precepts of Christ."[7]

In Britain in the early years of the twentieth century, the paternalistic and benevolent strain of Christian socialism gradually gave way to a more militant approach of largely Marxist inspiration. A dozen or more non-Marxist organizations, Anglican, Methodist, Baptist, and Roman Catholic, exerted some influence in different parts of the country, but none of them made a national impact. Although supported by such prominent churchmen as Archbishop William Temple (1881–1944) and R. H. Tawney (1880–1962), author of *The Acquisitive Society*, these movements never succeeded in breaking through the class barriers to attract significant numbers of workers as members. They consisted of do-gooders whose vision never extended to the point of conceiving that the workers could, and as the majority were entitled to, exercise the dominant role in society. In consequence, for all their good intentions, they continued to justify Marx's sneering comment that "Christian Socialism is but the holy water with which the priest consecrates the heart-burnings of the aristocrat."[8] The British Labour Party, founded in 1906, was the first organization to establish significant links with the workers.

The late 1930s and the 1940s, however, saw a significant revival of Christian socialism. In 1937, John MacMurray (1896–1976), Hewlett Johnson (1874–1966), and others visited Spain at the invitation of the republican government, and this delegation became the nucleus of the Christian Left. A professor of moral philosophy at the University of Edinburgh, MacMurray was the author of *Perspectives of Dialectical Materialism* and many other books. Johnson, popularly known as the "Red Dean of Canterbury," and MacMurray participated in 1941 in the Malvern Conference, at which Archbishop Temple presided. The Conference affirmed that "in our current situation we believe that to retain that part of the organization of society which allows the ownership of the principal resources of the country to remain in private hands entails the danger of making it more difficult for people to live according to the spirit of Christianity."[9] In 1945, Christian socialists, to the number of about a hundred, who were Labour Party members of the House of Commons formed a group which three years later published a statement entitled *In This Faith We Live*. In 1960, a number of small groups united to found the Christian Socialist movement. Their objectives, formulated in a pamphlet, *Papers from the Lamb*, were refined in 1981 in *Agenda for Prophets*. It proposed: the unity of all Christian people, especially in social purpose; reconciliation between nations; world peace with nuclear and general disarmament; redistribution to close gaps between rich and poor, and between rich and poor nations; common ownership and democratic control of the productive resources of the world; a classless society, combining social, sexual, and racial equality with personal responsibility and freedom of speech and association.[10]

France

In France, the outstanding figure was Philippe Buchez (1796–1865). In 1821 he helped found *La charbonnerie française*, which sought the overthrow of the Bourbons and the convocation of a national constituent assembly. In 1829 he was converted to Catholicism but did not practice because he hoped that by his nonobservance he would be more successful in reaching anticlerical republicans with his message of social Christianity. He believed that the ideals of the French Revolution were a development of the fundamental truths of Christianity. Distrusting the bourgeois government of Louis Philippe and deeply suspicious of the French bishops, he told the workers that they must assume the responsibility of changing their condition.

His proposed line of action was the creation of associations that would produce for their members, not for employers. Several such associations were in fact created. One, started in 1834, survived for some forty years. At its period of greatest development it had eight branches in Paris. For many years Buchez exercised a major influence on French workers and on the society in general. After the revolution of 1848, which put an end to the Orleans monarchy, the new national assembly chose him as its first president, recognizing him as the most highly qualified interpreter of a revolution that promised to bring about a reconciliation of the church and the people, an objective long sought by him.[11]

"We who have been elected by all," he said in his inaugural address, "are pledged to concern ourselves with all, and particularly with that class, the poor unfortunate part of the population, with which no one has ever before been concerned." The majority in the Assembly, however, as in the country, was conservative. Buchez quickly realized that they would not support his progressive ideas, and he withdrew from the presidency after one month in office. Almost immediately, the Assembly enacted antilabor legislation and provoked riots in Paris that were suppressed with the loss of thousands of lives. Not long afterward the Republic gave way to the dictatorship of the Second Empire.

Germany, Switzerland, Austria

Industrialization came later to Germany than to England and France, becoming significant only in the middle of the nineteenth century. The country was experiencing a rapid population growth, with an increase of 40 percent between 1815 and 1845, a phenomenon that increased poverty and emigration.

Wilhelm Weitling (1808–1871) was one of the first in the German-speaking world to advocate a Christian communist utopia, and he had considerable influence in both Germany and Austria. His principal work, which Marx called brilliant, was *Garantien der Harmonie und Freiheit* ["guarantees of harmony and freedom"]. In it he said that "more than a hundred places in the Bible" presented Jesus as a prophet of freedom and a forerunner of communism. For this statement he was charged with blasphemy, and spent sixteen months in jail. The threat of jail sentences, and in some jurisdictions of the death sentence, did not prevent extensive smuggling of this book from Switzerland into Austria and the German states. At a meeting of German exile socialists and communists in Brussels in 1846 at which Weitling was present, Marx attacked him for having incited German workers to revolt without having a sound basis in the form of strictly scientific ideas and concrete doctrine. The net result of such emotionally based activity, Marx argued, was to cause the workers simply to lose their jobs and their livelihood for no real gain. The meeting broke up without resolving the issue, but apparently the other participants sided with Marx. A few months later, Weitling left for New York, where he organized an association of German workers and established a commune near Dubuque, Iowa, a project that ended in bankruptcy in 1855.

Other important proponents of socialism in Germany were Christopher Blumhardt (1842–1919), Rudolf Todt (1839–1887), and Adolf Stoecker (1835–1909). "I am thinking of a completely new society," wrote Blumhardt, a Lutheran pastor.

I have thought that very soon now a religion would have no value if it did not transform society.... May the time come when we will succeed in giving society a new order, in which money will no longer be the principal object, but life and the happiness of men.... Where has Christ been present? Among the lowly. That is why they called him riff-raff, sinner. That was really what he was since he was a socialist. He took twelve proletarians and made them his disciples. Who then can accuse me of denying my Christian faith because I have chosen solidarity with proletarians and because I myself desire to be a proletarian?... Before God, there are no differences among men.... It is life lived in the spirit of Christ that has brought me to socialism.[12]

In *Der radicale deutsche Socialismus und die Cristliche Gesellschaft* ("radical German socialism and Christian society"), Todt condemned capitalism in the name of the Gospel, then asserted that true socialism must be based on Gospel principles.

Those who seek to understand the social question and contribute to its solution should have works on political economy at their right hand, works of scientific socialism at the left, and in front of them the open pages of the New Testament.... The socialist concepts of liberty, equality, and fraternity are an integral part of the Christian system; and the socialist concepts of solidarity of interests, cooperative production, and democracy have their entire base directly in the Bible, in the constitution and the customs of the church and in its apostolic teaching on these issues.[13]

In 1877 Todt joined Stoecker, a preacher at the imperial court, and a group of economists in founding the Evangelical Social Movement, which shortly developed into the Christian Social Workers Party. The role of this party was to create an alternative to the Social Democrats. It was not only antiliberal but also antisemitic, its position presented by Stoecker in a letter to Emperor William: "I don't attack the Jews; I only attack that kind of frivolous, atheistic, usurious, and deceiving Judaism that is the disgrace of our people." Although repudiated by major Protestant leaders, the Evangelical Social Movement had the support of Emperor William. "When challenged by an anarchistic and faithless party," he said, "the most efficacious defence of throne and altar consists in bringing the unbeliever back to Christianity and the church and in stressing Christian social thought more insistently than ever before."[14] The movement soon formulated two goals: a social goal that called for the organization of corporations of arts and crafts under government control; and a political goal, antiliberal, antisemitic, favoring an authoritarian government. This was precisely the program that Hitler would later implement with the corporatism of his totalitarian state.

A very different strand of socialism in the German-speaking world was centered in Switzerland, while influencing both Germany and Austria, in the first half of the twentieth century. Its most important figure was the theologian Karl Barth (1886–1968). By 1915 he had joined the Swiss Social Democratic Party and was preaching that Jesus is the movement for social justice and that Jesus rejected the concept of private property. "A real Christian must become a socialist if he is in earnest about the reformation of Christianity. A real socialist must be a Christian if he is earnest about the reformation of socialism."[15]

Paul Tillich (1886–1965) was also a member of the Social Democratic Party. As a chaplain on the Western Front during the First World War he had experienced a deep religious crisis. In 1919, in the turmoil of postwar Germany, he decided that this was the moment of Kairos, the day of salvation announced by St. Paul (2 Cor. 6:2). He founded the Kairos Circle, a discussion group, which started the *Journal of Religious Socialism*. In 1929 he was one of the founders of the *New Journal of Socialism*. It had dropped "religious" from the title but still referred to "spiritual and political formation" in the subtitle. Hitler suppressed it in 1933, and in the same year he had a book just published by Tillich, *The Socialist Decision*, confiscated. Tillich was dismissed from the faculty of the University of Frankfurt and moved to the United States to begin an even more illustrious theological career.

Both Barth and Tillich attempted to develop socialism starting from the *Bildung* ("intellectualism") that dominated both church and secular thinking and political activity in the German-speaking world. While criticizing the aristocratic intellectualism of their milieu, they were themselves dominated by it. They were armchair revolutionaries for whom the workers were objects of concern, not the subjects of their own liberation. It is not surprising that they never acquired a popular base.

Italy

Italy also saw small Christian socialist movements in the early twentieth century. The "worker" movement was promoted by some "socialist priests" in Reggio Emilia about 1904. In their newspaper, *La Plebe* ("the worker"), they presented their objective as "the christianizing of socialism and the socializing of Christianity, all in the name of Christ and following the directives of the Gospel." Supported by two groups of lay people, the radical Christians and the socialists, they quickly spread through Central Italy (Romagna, Marche, Campania). They failed, however, to gain the support of the Socialist Party, and the suspension from his priestly duties in August 1906 of their most prominent member, Rodrigo Levoni, because of involvement in politics without his bishop's approval, produced a crisis from which the movement did not recover.[16]

United States

Christian socialists in the United States were found almost exclusively in the Protestant denominations up to about 1950. It was only after that date that a significant Roman Catholic presence appeared. Late in the nineteenth century, some Protestant leaders began a hesitant approach to socialism in what became known as the Social Gospel Movement. This did not result from personal experience of deprivation but from religious motivation. It "did not grow out of actual suffering but rather out of moral and intellectual dissatisfaction with the suffering of others. . . . It pleaded for conversion, not revolt or withdrawal."[17] It saw individual selfishness, not an economic system (capitalism) as the primary cause of social problems.

Walter Rauschenbusch (1861–1918) represents the transition to openly professed socialism advocating it to the extent that it helped to usher in the Kingdom of God. "Atheism is in no way essential to Socialist thought," he wrote. "Socialists have no monopoly on it. It was the popular philosophy of continental liberalism in the '50's and '60's [of the nineteenth century], and the leaders of the working class absorbed it as true 'science.'... The Socialists found the Church against them, and thought God was against them too.... Whatever the sins of individual Socialists, they are tools in the hands of the Almighty."[18] Rauschenbusch joined the Christian Social Fellowship, an organization founded in 1906 "to permeate the churches,... to show that socialism is the economic expression of the religious life; to end the class struggle by establishing industrial democracy, and to hasten the reign of justice and brotherhood upon earth."[19] He refused, however, to join the Socialist Party of America, the first important socialist organization in the United States with a significant Christian input to its ideology. He did not believe, he said, either in "party socialism" (Socialist Party) or in "dogmatic socialism" (Marxism).[20]

Founded in 1901, the Socialist Party resulted from a breakaway from the Socialist Labor Party by followers of Eugene Debs (1855–1926), Morris Hilquist (1869–1933), Victor Berger (1860–1929), and George Herron (1862–1925). Herron, a Congregational minister, chaired the convention that brought together many factions to create a party that had a significant national impact for more than half a century. It had 120,000 dues-paying members in 1912, the year in which Debs received 6 percent of the presidential vote. Among the things for which Debs is remembered is his poem *Jesus*:

> The martyred Christ of the working class,
> the inspired evangel of the downtrodden masses,
> the world's supreme revolutionary leader,
> whose love for the poor and the children of the poor
> hallowed all the days of his consecrated life,
> lighted up and made forever holy
> the dark tragedy of his death,
> and gave to the ages his divine inspiration
> and his deathless name.[21]

In all, Debs ran five times for president on the Socialist ticket, and Norman Thomas (1884–1968), a Presbyterian minister who worked in an East Harlem church for seven years, ran six times. When he emerged as leader of the Socialist Party, Thomas gave it a new image, attracting middle-class intellectuals, including church people. The Party, nevertheless, never again reached the 6 percent of the presidential vote it received in 1912. Its role in national politics has long been marginal.

Herron was committed to a radical Christian socialism, seeing political socialism as a lever of social change. He agreed with Rauschenbusch that socialism was the ordained means to bring in the Kingdom of God proclaimed by Jesus. Socialism believes, he said, that "cooperative or harmonious organization of life is more practicable and liberating, more productive of the common good and of great individuality, than a competitive and individualistic organization. Jesus would call this the law of love. In modern economic terms, it is socialism."[22] Divorced and remarried in 1901, Herron was deposed from the Congregational ministry. He later renounced Christianity.

The most outstanding woman proponent of socialism in the United States in the nineteenth century was Frances Willard (1839–1898). A native of Wisconsin, she built the Women's Christian Temperance Union into a national movement with two hundred thousand dues-paying members. Elected Union president in 1879, she broadened the interests and objectives of the Union beyond temperance to the promotion of women's suffrage, and she insisted that religion must be concerned with material as well as spiritual welfare. Within a decade she "transformed the organization from a holy crusade against drink into a social movement with far-reaching aspirations."[23] By 1893 she was interpreting this crusade to mean that capitalism should be replaced by socialism. In her presidential address in that year she asserted that "in every Christian there exists a socialist, and in every socialist a Christian."[24] The Women's Temperance Union succeeded in bringing together women of very different backgrounds, old-American middle-class Protestants, working-class or frontier farm women, and immigrant working-class women.[25]

Two Christian socialist organizations were created in the United States in the early part of the twentieth century, the Protestant interdenominational Christian Socialist Fellowship organized at Louisville, Kentucky, in 1906, and the Church Socialist League, an Episcopal group formed in 1911. Neither organization was affiliated to the Socialist Party but many members of both were members of that party. From 1914 to 1924 the League published a quarterly, *The Social Preparation*, at Utica and Geneva, New York. The Fellowship published *The Christian Socialist* in Chicago. It appeared weekly at times, monthly at other times. In its April 1, 1914, issue it defined the "one, great, specific purpose" of the Fellowship as "to permeate the churches and other religious organizations with the social message of Jesus, which in an age of machine production means Socialism, and nothing else." During the bitter industrial conflicts of the years preceding the First World War, conflicts in which the employers often used goons against strikers, it was militantly loyal to the workers. One of the worst incidents was the Ludlow massacre in 1913, when Colorado National Guardsmen, their salaries paid by a Rockefeller company, shot to death thirteen striking workers at a Rockefeller-owned coal mine and started a fire in the workers' makeshift quarters in which eleven children and two mothers burned to death. "Contemptible as Rockefeller is," *The Christian Socialist* editorialized, "he acts strictly in accordance with capitalist morality."[26]

Most Christian socialists in the United States in the first part of the twentieth century joined the Christian Social Fellowship. Members had to belong both to a church and a socialist party, and "where possible" also to a trade union. The Fellowship's publication, *The Christian Socialist*, achieved a readership of over nineteen thousand. As evaluated by H. Richard Niebuhr, the Fellowship emphasized the opposition between Christ and culture, portraying Jesus as a revolutionary figure who sided with the oppressed.[27] Membership was, however, overwhelmingly middle-class, and when the Socialist Party condemned U.S. participation in World War I, the Christian socialists found their national allegiance stronger than their class commitment. It was not until the Great Depression that they reformed as the Fellowship of Socialist Christians, led by Reinhold Niebuhr (1892–1971). By changing the designation of "Christian socialists" to "socialist Christians," Niebuhr explained, they were stressing two things: that their primary loyalty was to the Christian faith; and that they were not a particular brand of socialists. Niebuhr agreed with Marx on the inevitability of a new social order. His Calvinistic theology of the depravity of human nature, however, did not allow him to share Marx's optimism regarding the nature of that order. In addition, by the late 1930s, both he and the Fellowship had shifted their orientations significantly from commitment to the struggle for socialism to Roosevelt's New Deal. When World War II broke out in Europe in 1939, they rejected the pacifist stance of the Socialist Party as utopian in its standards of judgment and misguided in its analysis. A generation would pass before there would develop again any significant interest in socialism among U.S. Protestants.

Of the many Protestant luminaries who identified themselves as socialists, the most distinguished were Walter Rauschenbusch, and — for a time — Reinhold Niebuhr. But most of the European immigrants who formed the vast majority of the Socialist Party militants in its heyday were hardline enemies of religion. Their antireligion bias was further strengthened by the attitude of the Catholic church. Its leadership did indeed support the trade union movement, even at a time when Rome frowned on it. But it was the nonideological unionism concerned exclusively with material benefits for the members which alone has flourished in the United States. The Catholics consistently opposed all political movements calling for revolutionary social change. They followed Pope Leo XIII's claim that the right of property is sanctioned by the natural law and listened to Pope Pius XI when he told them that God had determined that there should be rich people and poor people in the world so that virtues may be exercised and merits proven.

The most vocal religious socialists in the United States today are members of the Religion and Socialism Commission of the Democratic Socialists of America, a wing of the Democratic Party. Until his death in 1989, Michael Harrington cop-chaired the commission with Barbara Ehrenreich. Author of *The Other America* and many studies of socialism and poverty, Harrington was long active in the Catholic Worker movement. Commission members include James Luther Adams, James Cone, Harvey Cox, Arthur McGovern, Rosemary Ruether, Dorothee Sölle, Arthur Waskow, and Cornel West. Since 1977 it has published the quarterly *Religious Socialism*.

•

Pyotr Alexandrovitch Miüsov, a character in Fyodor Mikhailovich Dostoevsky's *Brothers Karamazov*, extolled the contribution
of Christians to the socialist movement in these words: "We are
not particularly afraid of all these socialists, anarchists, infidels,
and revolutionists; we keep watch on them and know all their
goings on. But there are a few peculiar men among them who
believe in God and are Christians, but at the same time are socialists. Those are the people we are most afraid of. They are dreadful
people."[28]

The history of Christian socialism described in this chapter
does not support Dostoevsky. On the contrary, the regimes claiming to be socialist or to be building socialism that now rule a
third of the people of the world are almost all inspired by the
antireligious or nonreligious movements he dismisses as unimportant. Later chapters, however, will explore more recent Christian
movements that approach Marx not as an enemy but as an ally.
One cannot exclude the possibility that they will justify Dostoevsky's evaluation. It is certainly noteworthy that in the United
States in the 1980s the religious Left has to a great extent replaced the secular Left as the leading advocate of radical social
change. This major development was stressed by Michael Ferber,
assistant director of the Washington-based Coalition for a New
Foreign and Military Policy, in an article entitled "Politics of Transcendence: Religious Revival on the Left." The secular Left, he
wrote, must recognize that "the religious Left is the only Left
we've got"; and that "churches and synagogues provide a space
that is relatively untouched by the commercialization of the larger
society." He attributes the decline of the secular Left to its ig-
noring of an area that is important to the religious Left, namely,
values.

"Socialists have neglected the terrain that churches occupy,"
he concludes,

a terrain which, for lack of serious thinking and acting on it by the Left,
may be relinquished to the political Right, which has done a good job
of claiming it. It is our task to talk values, to talk ideals, to talk transcendence. We must recover some of our own lost traditions — such
as the Romantic rebellion against early industrial capitalism — which

were infused with moral and religious themes. If we have a vision, we should be open advocates of it and not be put off by dismissive remarks that it is utopian and unscientific, that it is religious and unrealistic or impractical.[29]

Chapter 4

Christians for Socialism

Chile in 1970 created a new challenge for Christians when a party committed to establishing a socialist society won an election that brought it constitutionally to power. The event should be seen, not in isolation, but in the historic context in which it occurred. Many new possibilities for socialism were opening up around the world. The Soviet Union had begun the process of de-Stalinization, a process that would in due course lead to the *perestroika* and *glasnost* of Gorbachev.

Encouraged by the changes in the Catholic church brought about by Vatican Council II, as well as by parallel processes in the many Protestant churches that were members of the World Council of Churches, Marxist leaders in many countries, especially in Italy, France, and Czechoslovakia, had embarked on re-examination of their presuppositions and were discussing the possibilities of dialogue and even of cooperation with Christians. The student revolts on both sides of the Atlantic in 1968 had shaken basic assumptions in the dominant capitalist countries. And in many parts of Latin America and elsewhere in the Third World, grassroots guerrilla movements were marking the emergence of the poor as a subject, no longer merely a victim, of history.

The Latin American Context

The specific response to Chile's new historic situation in 1970 must be seen within the cultural context of Latin America, a region for centuries peripheral to and heavily dependent on the dominant capitalist powers. Both Christianity and Marxism were imported from Europe, looked to Europe for ideological guidance, and responded instinctively to changes in their respective European fountainheads, namely, Rome and Moscow. The difference, of course, was that communist parties were relatively new in most countries, having been aggressively promoted in the two decades following the creation of the Third International in 1919, while Christianity had had five centuries in which to put down deep roots in peasantry and workers alike.

Socialist movements on a small scale began in Argentina, Brazil, Mexico, and elsewhere in Latin America in the middle of the nineteenth century. The first party of socialist inspiration was Chile's Democratic Party, founded in 1887. Argentina elected a socialist deputy to parliament in 1904. Following the 1919 formation of the Third International, with its detailed conditions for recognition of a party as "communist," official parties multiplied: the United States in 1919; Uruguay, in 1920; Brazil, Chile, and Guatemala, in 1922; Cuba, in 1925; Colombia, in 1930; and Venezuela, in 1931. It was about this time that Latin America's only significant Marxist theoretician began to cause problems for the Comintern dogmatists. He was José Carlos Mariátegui (1894–1930), and his insistence on the importance of the indigenous rural worker in Peru, as well as on the positive role of nationalism, ran against the antipeasant and internationalist line then being vigorously pursued by Stalin. The challenge of Hugo Blanco's mobilization of peasants in Peru in the 1970s and of Sendero Luminoso and other indigenous movements in that country in the 1980s would confirm the accuracy of Mariátegui's analysis.

It was not till the late 1920s that a parallel organization of Catholics, similarly stimulated by European events, began. Given the ideological rigidity that marked Stalin's rise to power, the Catholic initiatives developed not only without connection with but in positive opposition to the spread of socialist ideas and parties. Pope Pius XI was promoting in Italy the creation of regimented organizations of the laity under the name of Catholic Action, and this was the structure introduced to Uruguay in 1929, to Argentina in 1930, and within a few years to all of Latin America.

Both Catholic and Marxist movements were overwhelmingly middle-class. The Communist Parties, following the sinuous path of Stalin's Russia, committed themselves after 1935 to support of the Popular Front, switched to a defense of the Hitler-Stalin Pact in 1939, and reversed their stand once more when Hitler invaded Russia in 1941. By war's end in 1945 they were completely discredited everywhere in Latin America, with the possible exception of Chile, in which the Party had kept closer links with labor and had a stronger popular base. But even in Chile, the Communist Party had lost and would not regain its position as leader of the revolutionary left.

During these decades of the 1940s and 1950s the movement of Catholic Action was in the contrary direction. The Falange was created in Chile in 1936 by members of Catholic University Youth led by Eduardo Frei and inspired by Manuel Larraín, a priest who would become bishop of Talca, president of the Latin American Bishops' Council (CELAM), and a zealous supporter of Pope John XXIII's *aggiornamento* ("updating") of the church. Similar political formations grew out of Catholic Action in all Latin America. Influenced by Franco's Spain and Salazar's Portugal, they were politically populist, in full sympathy with the anti-imperialist and antiliberal bourgeoisie, envisaging social reform that would introduce a neo-Christendom.

Other European influences made themselves felt after World War II. Louis Lebret, a French Dominican priest, founder of the Economics and Humanism group and of the Institute for Research and Training for Development (Paris), devoted much time to observing and analyzing social conditions in Latin America in the late 1940s and 1950s. His humanist approach, stressing the importance of being rather than merely having, influenced many Latin Americans, as did his assertion that the first task was "to develop the whole man and all men through general economic progress."[1]

Meanwhile, a Belgian priest sociologist, François Houtart, was editing a forty-eight-volume work, the first sociological study ever of the Catholic church in Latin America. As early as 1956, he was urging people to recognize that "a silent revolution" had begun and that the church could ignore it at its peril. He pointed out that social movements of Christian inspiration were penetrating Latin

America from Europe, including the first Christian Democratic parties (in Peru and Guatemala). Even though the Christian Democrat program was essentially defensive, seeking to anticipate revolution by cosmetic reforms, it marked the commitment of Christians to a social and political struggle, legitimating an approach that could be taken to effect radical change.

Winds of Change

New dynamic elements appeared in 1959 with the coming to power of Castro in Cuba and Pope John XXIII's announcement that he was going to call a General Council. Khrushchev had by then begun to unmask Stalin, and popular opposition was rising throughout Latin America to the U.S. model of dependent capitalism. Populism was in total crisis. The first shock was the overthrow of Arbenz in Guatemala in 1954, a U.S. misjudgment based on its misinterpretation of populism as communism, an error for which Central America is still paying dearly. In the same year Vargas committed suicide in Brazil. Perón fell in Argentina in 1955, as did Rojas Pinilla in Colombia and Pérez Jiménez in Venezuela in 1957, and Batista in Cuba in 1959.

It was a concrete historical context in which progressive Christians and Marxists found themselves faced with the same option. Che Guevara and Camilo Torres formulated it in identical terms: a Latin American revolution that would go beyond capitalism and bring the people to power. At the level of theory or ideology the two were diametrically opposed, a confirmed Marxist and a Catholic priest who insisted publicly that he was not a Marxist. What united them was their commitment to the people, a commitment that led both of them to a quixotic gesture. It cost them their lives and seemed to have ended all prospect of cooperation between Christians and Marxists.

Christians in Brazil, however, tried a different path. Popular Action, founded in 1962 by Luis Alberto Gomes de Souza and others, was the first Christian grouping in Latin America with a professed socialist and Marxist approach. Its members, in common with the communists and the populists, were persecuted — many killed, others tortured, others exiled — under the military dictatorship that seized power in 1964. This marked the transition from the theory of developmentalism to the National Security State not only in Brazil but soon in most of Latin America, a system that lumped together all revolutionaries, Christian or Marxist, and which in consequence brought the two emotionally closer.

Christians were also encouraged to take a new look at the hitherto apparently monolithic Soviet position by Khrushchev's open repudiation of Stalinism. At the twentieth congress of Russia's Communist Party in February 1956, Khrushchev astonished Russians and people all over the world by declaring that the Central Committee of the Communist Party had "vigorously condemned the cult of the individual as being alien to the spirit of Marxism-Leninism" and equally condemned "making a particular leader the hero and miracle worker," and the twenty-second Congress of the Soviet Communist Party reaffirmed this position in 1961.[2] Marxists, for their part, were favorably impressed by the renewal of the Catholic church at Vatican Council II (1962–1965), a renewal formalized for Latin America at the 1968 meeting in Medellín of the bishops of the hemisphere.

By the time of the Medellín meeting of bishops, a radical change had occurred in Catholic-Protestant relations. Less than a decade earlier, the executive committee of CELAM, meeting at Fomeque, Colombia, had identified its principal enemies as Protestantism, communism, spiritism, and Masonry. In this they were repeating their longstanding complaint that Protestantism's objective was to destroy the Catholic church. That attitude changed only when significant groups on both sides became committed to social change. A pioneer in promoting such change was Richard Shaull, a North American Protestant theologian. He had already had had twenty years' experience in Latin America when in 1952 he presented a paper in Buenos Aires on "Christians and Revolution." Ten years later he joined other Protestant theologians and social scientists to form *Iglesia y Sociedad en América Latina* (ISAL: "Church and Society in Latin America").

ISAL from its beginning stressed the close relation of development to humanization. It supported the ongoing Latin American revolution, while insisting that what was needed was not a "Christian answer" but participation of Christians in the revolutionary process.[3] ISAL quickly established close working relations with likeminded Catholic theologians and social scientists, and before long it opened its membership to Catholics. Its input to the documents of the Medellín meeting of Latin America's Catholic bishops in 1968, though informal, was substantial. These ISAL initiatives were encouraged and supported by parallel developments in the World Council of Churches: its fourth plenary meeting at Uppsala in 1968, with the theme, "God makes all things new," the proclamation of an eschatology beginning from now; the establishment by the World Council and the Vatican of an agency to study Third World problems. This Committee on Society, Development, and Peace (SODEPAX) was an expression of the commitment of the Christian churches to seek jointly to create a better world and a more human society.

Ecumenism in Latin America thus involved a process quite different from that of Europe at the same time. It began, not with dialogue conducted by theoreticians seeking points of agreement and distinguishing between what was essential and peripheral in the positions of each side, but with working together in pursuit of common goals. This new type of ecumenism no longer demanded theological consensus as a necessary preliminary to a common commitment to the oppressed Latin American masses. In a very short time it produced a radical change in the religious configuration of the hemisphere. Where formerly there had been an emotional gulf and institutional conflict between Protestants on one side and Catholics on the other, now we have Catholics and Protestants committed to radical social change living and working together on one side, and on the other Catholics and Protestants supportive of the status quo at least tactically united in pursuit of their political objectives.[4]

At the same time as this momentous change was taking place within the Christian denominations in Latin America, new groups were forming on the Left. They rejected the Soviet interpretation of Marx in favor of Trotskyite, Maoist, or Guevarist models, and they ceased to identify with the old Communist Parties, almost all of which had lost their revolutionary enthusiasm and sunk into bourgeois respectability. Following Castro's ascent to power in Cuba in 1959, a guerrilla movement appeared in Guatemala in 1961, and in the same year the Sandinista Front was formed in Nicaragua.

Venezuela saw a guerrilla movement in 1962. In Colombia the Republic of Marquetalia was established in 1964, by which time guerrilla movements had started in Peru, Paraguay, Honduras, Ecuador, and Brazil.

Many of these groups represented a radical change in that their membership was drawn in large part from the ranks of University Catholic Youth. They included the Montoñero leader Mario Firmenich in Argentina and the equally distinguished member of Bolivia's Teoponte guerrillas, Nestor Paz. All of them, whatever their ideological starting point, learned in the mountains to identify with the aspirations of the *campesinos* who constituted their logistical support base. They also learned to recognize the determining role played in the lives and value systems of the *campesinos* by the popular religion they have maintained through a score of generations.

Medellín

As the Left was beginning to identify popular religion as an ally, Christian intellectuals were also making important discoveries. Priests, nuns, and other pastoral agents were learning from their contacts with the masses in urban slums and in the countryside that the steady deterioration in social conditions called for new priorities and also for new tools to interpret reality and provide remedies. By the late 1960s they were convinced that the reformist project institutionalized in 1961 in the Alliance for Progress, and at first eagerly embraced and supported by them, was not working and could not work. By 1965 a theory of dependency had been formulated by Argentine economist Raúl Prebisch and others to challenge the conventional theory of development. It related organically the poverty of the poor, both of poor individuals and poor nations, with the wealth of the rich. The poor were poor because the rich had made them poor and kept them poor by appropriating to themselves the lion's share of the surplus value created by the poor. This formulation, derived from the Marxist analysis of reality, was affirmed by the bishops of Latin America at Medellín 1968, when they identified external neocolonialism, international monopolies, and the international imperialism of money as the principal causes of the economic dependence of the hemisphere.

By this time both Catholic and Protestant theologians were openly using the Marxist analysis, and in fact Protestant theologians participated with their Catholic colleagues in drafting the preliminary Medellín documents. Another significant influence on Medellín was Pope Paul's encyclical, *Populorum Progressio* (April 1968) in which the pope declared that "development is the new name for peace."

The most striking advance in the social analysis of Medellín is found in the Document on Peace.

We refer here particularly to the implications for our countries of dependence on a center of economic power, around which they gravitate. For this reason, our nations frequently do not own the goods or have a say in economic decisions affecting them. It is obvious that this will not fail to have political consequences, given the interdependence of these two fields. . . . Because of the relative depreciation of the terms of exchange, the value of raw materials is increasingly less in relation to the cost of manufactured products. This means that the countries which produce raw materials — especially if they are dependent on one major export — always remain poor, while the industrialized countries enrich themselves. This injustice, clearly denounced by *Populorum Progressio*, nullifies the eventual positive effect of external aid and constitutes a permanent menace to peace. . . . The principal guilt for economic dependence of our countries rests with powers, inspired by uncontrolled desire for gain, which leads to economic dictatorship and the "international imperialism of money" condemned by Pope Pius XI in *Quadragesimo Anno* and by Pope Paul VI in *Populorum Progressio*.[5]

The bishops followed the social analysis with a doctrinal reflection. Oppression by power groups, they said, might give the impression of maintaining peace and order; but in reality it was nothing but "the continuous and inevitable seed of rebellion and war," because "peace can only be obtained by creating a new order which carries with it a more perfect justice among men."[6] Latin America, they continued,

in many instances finds itself faced with a situation of injustice that can be called institutionalized violence, when, because of a structural deficiency of industry and agriculture, of national and international economy, of cultural and political life, "whole towns lack necessities, live in such dependence as hinders all initiative and responsibility as well as possibility for cultural promotion and participation in social and political life" (*Populorum Progressio*, no. 30) thus violating fundamental rights. This situation demands all-embracing, courageous, urgent, and profoundly renovating transformations. We should not be surprised, therefore, that the "temptation to violence" is surfacing in Latin America. One should not abuse the patience of a people that for years has borne a situation that would not be acceptable to any one with any degree of awareness of human rights.[7]

About the time of the Medellín meeting, the issue of Marxist infiltration of Christian thought burst into the open at the Latin American Institute of Economic and Social Studies, ILADES, a Jesuit-sponsored center for study of the social sciences, in Santiago, Chile. In the charged atmosphere of a presidential campaign, two European Jesuits, Pierre Bigo and Roger Vekemans, publicly criticized Gonzalo Arroyo, a Chilean Jesuit, and Franz Hinkelammert, for supporting the Socialist Party, headed by Salvador Allende. Catholics, they argued, could not support a political party that professed Marxist principles. In December 1969, the bishops of Chile shut down ILADES, but without publicly expressing a view on the issues. When Allende became president in 1970, Bigo and Vekemans withdrew, Vekemans joining Bishop (now Cardinal) Alfonso López Trujillo, then secretary general of CELAM, in Bogotá, Colombia, to continue the war against Marxist influence in the church in Latin America. Three years later, with the overthrow of Allende, it was the turn of Arroyo and Hinkelammert to go into exile.[8]

Santiago, 1972

During the late 1960s and early 1970s, movements were formed in many parts of Latin America by progressive priests who were soon joined by nuns and lay people, and in many cases also by Protestant sympathizers. Their specific purposes varied according to local problems, but their general thrust identified them as critical of capitalism and favorable to some form of socialism. They included Golconda in Colombia, headed by Bishop Geraldo Valencia, Third World Priests in Argentina, ONIS in Peru, The Eighty, the Young Church and later Christians for Socialism in Chile, Priests for the People in Mexico, the Quito Reflection Group in Ecuador, and Christians for Socialism headed by Bishop Antonio Parrilla in Puerto Rico.

In April 1971, eighty priests living in Chile and pastorally involved with working-class people, published the Declaration of The Eighty. Both the themes and the methodology of The Eighty showed a high level of analysis of Chilean reality. They accepted praxis rather than general, abstract principles as their starting point. They adopted Marxism as the best means to illuminate this political praxis. They asserted the compatibility of Christianity and Marxist socialism. Both sides, they insisted, must overcome historical prejudices, accept their respective traditions, and go beyond an exclusively economic reading of history. The united masses of the people had to be mobilized for the construction of socialism, a project that called for political work among the masses of peasants and workers who were not yet incorporated into the socialist process because they were controlled economically, politically, and culturally — especially through the Christian Democrats and the institutional church — by the dominant bourgeois classes.

The final statement denounced the exploitation, poverty, and cultural deprivation resulting from "domination by foreign imperialism and maintained by the ruling classes." It affirmed a commitment to the socialist process under way in Allende's Chile and called for an end to the prejudice and mistrust that divide Christians and Marxists.

To Marxists we say that authentic religion is not the opiate of the people. It is, on the contrary, a liberating stimulus to revivify and renew the world constantly. To Christians we offer a reminder that our God has been and is committed personally to the history of human beings.... This collaboration will be facilitated to the extent that two things are done: (1) to the extent that Marxism presents itself more and more as an instrument for analyzing and transforming society; (2) to the extent that we Christians proceed to purify our faith of everything that prevents us from shouldering real and effective commitment.[9]

Fidel Castro, when he visited Chile eight months later, responded enthusiastically as a Marxist to this overture. "I believe," he told The Eighty, "that we have reached a moment in which religion can enter the political arena in regard to man and his material needs.... I say there are ten times, ten thousand times more points of agreement between Christianity and socialism and communism than between Christianity and capitalism."[10]

The movement of Christians for Socialism formally began in April 1972 with the Encounter of Christians for Socialism in Santiago, Chile, organized by The Eighty. The more than four hundred delegates had come from Argentina, Bolivia, Brazil, Colombia, Costa Rica, Cuba, Dominican Republic, Ecuador, Haiti, Mexico, Nicaragua, Panama, Paraguay, Peru, Puerto Rico, and Uruguay. They included 170 Catholic priests, 30 nuns, 160 lay Catholics, and 40 Protestant laity and pastors. Christians and Marxists need each other, Gonzalo Arroyo told the meeting:

An objective analysis of the political reality of Latin America makes it clear that the repeated failures of the Left to attract the masses to a committed struggle against the national and international forces of capitalism demand the incorporation of Christians on a massive scale into the revolutionary process. But the Christian also sees clearly that his political practice cannot be deduced directly from his faith.... When fighting for a more just and more human society, the revolutionary Christian has recourse to science and revolutionary theory in order to open up historical roads for his activity alongside the working class and the people of Latin America. As Che said: "When Christians will run the risk of making a full revolutionary testimony, the Latin American revolution will be invincible."[11]

The final document represented a further development of themes presented at Medellín. Vigorous rejection of "a Christian social third way" between capitalism and socialism reflected the political option in Chile between Frei's Christian Democracy and Allende's socialism. "The sharpening of the class struggle," it said, "excludes any kind of presumed neutrality or apoliticism." Repeating the expression used by Castro in his talk to The Eighty the previous year, they noted a growing consciousness of the need for "a strategic alliance" between revolutionary Christians and Marxists. Insisting that Christianity "is included in the confrontation between exploited and exploiters," they said that theology needs a socio-analytical tool, and that the Bible must be read in a new way that does not block Christian commitment to the revolutionary process.[12]

Europe

The Santiago meeting quickly inspired similar movements in many parts of the world. A document drawn up by two hundred Spanish Christians, clergy and laity, in January 1973 closely followed the Santiago statement. It said that the real contradictions of the Gospel message are found, not in Marxism, but "in capitalist materialism based on the profit motive, consumerism, and individual advantage." The congress was held in Calofell, Catalonia, but because of the need for clandestinity under the Franco regime, the documents were signed as coming from Avila. A second congress was held in September 1975 in Cornella, Barcelona, with Burgos as the cover city. More than six hundred persons attended the third congress, held in semi-clandestinity near Madrid in March 1977. A sociological analysis of the movement presented at this congress identified it as composed of blue-collar workers and farm laborers, union leaders, university students, and white-collar workers. Most members were militants in the Socialist, Communist, or New Left Parties. At the time of this last meeting, more than four hundred Christians, including twelve priests, were registered and active members of the Spanish Communist Party in Madrid.[13]

In Italy in April 1972, a number of priests and laypeople who were disappointed that the 1971 Synod of Bishops had failed to promote reform of the Roman Curia founded the November 7 Movement. It took its name from the date on which the Synod ended. Its first congress, held in November, denounced the Vatican for using the Italian state as its secular arm. A second meeting in Florence the following month, sponsored by twelve radical Italian periodicals — eleven Catholic and one Protestant — decided on an activist policy in the working-class struggle for social justice. A primary motivation for the promoters of this movement was their belief that social reform in Italy required the ending of the Vatican involvement in Italian politics, an involvement institutionalized in the Christian Democrat Party.[14] Under the name of Christians for Socialism, they held two national congresses, one at Bologna in September 1973 and one at Naples in November 1974.

More than two thousand Christians from all parts of Italy met at Bologna. They rejected the ideology of the Christian Democrats as calculated to support conservatism and defend the interests of oppressive capitalism. They criticized the church for having become an integral part of the capitalist system, supporting the Christian Democrats and keeping the Catholic world in a situation of religious underdevelopment. Reaffirming the political pluralism of Catholics, they rejected any kind of integralism of faith and politics, even of the Left, on the ground that political activity has its own integrity.

The Naples congress, with twenty-five hundred participants, included a discussion of the relationship between faith and politics. Speakers included Giovanni Franzoni, Giulio Girardi, Raniero La Valle, Sergio Ribet, Sandro Antoniazzi, and Marco Bisceglia. Girardi argued for the dialectical unity of Christianity and Marxism. La Valle, while favoring a working agreement between the two, emphasized the transcendence of faith. Each position found equal support, and the final document limited itself to asserting that "for us faith is not subordinated to politics, nor politics to faith; faith and politics are neither identified with each other nor do they make each other superfluous."

In Portugal, a Christians for Socialism movement developed after the 1974 revolution. At a meeting in Lisbon in January 1975, it criticized the "ecclesiastical ideological apparatus" for having been Portuguese fascism's greatest ally. It called for an ideological debate within the church itself on the role of religion as a support of capitalism, and a reinterpretation of the Gospel as the message of true liberation of the exploited classes. The Marxist input was specifically acknowledged:

Christians for Socialism are, above all, Christians who, at the level of their social expressions, affirm and fight for the construction of a society where there will be no exploiters and exploited, where there will be no exploitation of some persons by other persons. For this purpose they intend to use Marxist methodology, but their members can and must make political choices within these parameters, in different organizations and parties.[15]

Similar groups were forming about this time in other Western European countries. Spanish migrant workers from many countries of Western Europe formed a chapter of Christians for Socialism at a meeting in Luxembourg in May 1974. Also in 1974, a group was established in Holland on the initiative of the Student Christian movement. Its membership included the radical priests and ministers of an organization called Septuagint and Dutch priests from Chile who had named themselves Christians for Socialism in Exile. In April 1975 French-speaking Belgians formed a chapter at Namur. In France, more than four hundred took part in a conference on Faith, Christian Communities, and Socialism, at Orleans, in June 1976. The Communist Party, the Socialist Party, and the United Socialist Party sent observers. Smaller movements, often in the form of study groups, developed in West Germany, the Netherlands, Denmark, and Britain. Most of the participants in West Germany were from Protestant traditions. Their conference resulted in significant contributions to the discussion of the relationship of Christian faith and Marxist socialism.

United States

In the United States, in early 1974, Christians of different denominations, who had worked as missionaries in Latin America, began a reflection and action group which developed into an organization with a socialist perspective and analysis. Its ambitions included establishing contacts with the U.S. working class and supporting Christians involved in political action within a socialist perspective. It was also committed to working within the Christian churches, confronting them when they obscured the exploitative nature of capitalism. Such work, they hoped, would develop and articulate a Christian religious experience growing out of Jesus' identification with the poor and oppressed. It would thus support a socialist political perspective and deepen the commitment to the struggle for justice.

The group called itself ACTS, a name intended to recall Acts 4:32: "The whole group of believers was united in heart and soul: no one claimed for his own use anything he had, as everything was held in common." Many interpreted the name as an acronym,

American Christians Toward Socialism, and this became the accepted title.

In May 1975, ACTS participated in the First International Encounter of Christians for Socialism in Quebec, Canada, contributing a report on the state of church and society in the United States. National reports were also presented by groups from Chile, Peru, Colombia, Ecuador, Mexico, Cuba, Puerto Rico, Spain, Italy, Belgium, Netherlands, West Germany, Britain, and France. The meeting focused on the international dimension of the present phase of capitalism, characterized by the dominance of the transnationals, the increasingly fascist tendencies of "democratic" regimes, and the transnational character of cultural power. It stressed the need for new forms of faith and church life as alternatives to those of the institutional church.

"Today the world is suffering from an economic crisis," the final document declared,

but the oppressed classes always live in crisis.... The profound cause of the crisis is the unequal and contradictory character which expansionist world capitalism has assumed. Its tendency is characterized by a concentration of capital and technology in the hands of transnational corporations. The majority of these corporations operate from headquarters in the United States and are supported by that country's government, invading practically the entire world through their affiliates. The power of these corporations is greater than that of many nations.... Within the contradictions of the capitalist countries,... another type of social organization is possible and is already being put into practice. Socialism is the historic movement which brings together those who have made a class option in favor of the interest of workers and of the world's most oppressed peoples.... Hitherto the faith has been lived and understood in isolation from the contemporary revolutionary struggle and in a world to which a conflictual and dialectical vision of history is alien. Insofar as identification with the struggles and interests of the popular classes constitutes for the Christian the axis of a new way of being human and accepting the gift of God's word, to that degree the Christian becomes aware that a faith-reflection rooted in historical praxis is really a theology linked to the liberation struggles of the oppressed.[16]

Four months later ACTS convoked a national conference at Detroit under the joint sponsorship of the Latin American Division of the United States Catholic Conference and the Latin American Working Group of the National Council of Churches. Some sixty "reflection groups" all around the United States had spent several months attempting to develop a deep and informed analysis of the nation's sociohistorical experience. Their evaluations helped the planning committee to prepare the agenda. Issues raised included the origin and functioning of industrial capitalism as an economic and as an ideological system, the nature of class differences in the United States, the economic and psychic roots of racism and sexism, the nature of the relationship between the rich and the poor countries, and the ideological uses of religion in the United States.

It was the consensus of the meeting that no official conclusions should be formulated but instead that members should be encouraged to pursue the issues that had been raised. It also became clear, thanks especially to the participation of leading Latin American theologians, that the Christians for Socialism movement could no longer be envisaged independently from the theology of liberation. The development and significance of that theology are the subject of a later chapter. But first it is appropriate to examine the parallel evolution of Marxism and the efforts on both sides to determine if and to what extent its worldview is compatible with that of Christianity.

Chapter 5

Christian-Marxist Dialogue
in Europe

Pope John XXIII, in *Pacem in Terris*, distinguished between false philosophical systems regarding the "nature, origin, and destiny of the universe," and historical movements with "economic, social, cultural, or political ends" that have originated from these teachings and still draw inspiration from them. Such movements, he continued, can "contain elements that are positive and deserving of approval."

Everyone understood that the reference was to Marxist socialism. For Catholics the way was opened to explore possibilities for collaboration. Cardinal Franziscus Koenig, president of the Vatican Secretariat for Non-Believers, is one who spelled this out very precisely. "To what extent Marxism is, by its nature, bound up with atheism," he has written, "ought to be deduced, not only from an analysis of Marxism itself, but also very largely from the evolution of Marxist states in the political sphere."[1]

Eurocommunism

Various Communist Parties in Western Europe also quickly responded to Pope John's overture. They were able to do so because by the mid-1950s Moscow had lost the absolute control it had previously exercised over the parties outside the Soviet sphere of influence. The change had resulted from a combination of factors:

the Soviet Union's decision to promote "peaceful coexistence," Khrushchev's report to the Twentieth Party Congress on Stalin's crimes, and the Sino-Soviet split.

The assertions of independence by West European parties were for a time generically called "neocommunism." Some observers, however, criticized the term as implying that the changes were substantive, that a qualitatively different kind of communism had come into existence, although it was far from clear that the changes were more than tactical. In 1975, a Yugoslav journalist, Frane Barbieri, coined the term "Eurocommunism" as an abbreviation for Western European communism; and this term was gradually accepted both by observers and by the parties themselves, leaving it to history to determine the nature of the changes.[2] The extent to which these national communist movements openly repudiate Soviet leadership varies, but all of them have distanced themselves significantly from rigid Marxism-Leninism. All are committed to peaceful — though still "revolutionary" — transformation of society. The first major public break with Moscow was their 1968 condemnation of the Soviet-led occupation of Czechoslovakia. Later came criticism of violations of civil liberty, psychiatric imprisonment of political dissidents, forced labor camps, and other features of the Soviet system.

Already in 1962, the year before *Pacem in Terris*, the Italian Communist Party had put out feelers. "Experience confirms," it stated, "that the Christian conscience, faced with the dramatic reality of the contemporary world, can serve to stimulate a commitment to struggle for the socialist transformation of society." The invitation became more attractive in 1969 when Enrico Berlinguer, as spokesman of the Italian Party at a conference of seventy-five communist and worker parties in Moscow, openly distanced himself from the Soviet model. The Italian is the biggest communist party outside the Soviet bloc and consistently receives at least a quarter of the votes in Italian elections.

"We reject the idea that there can be a single model of socialist society valid for all situations," Berlinguer said. "Our united struggle . . . is geared to realizing a new socialist society, which will guarantee all freedoms — personal and collective, civil and religious — the nonideological character of the state, the possibility for different parties to exist side by side, and pluralism in society, culture, and ideals." He specifically affirmed the Italian Party's disagreement with Moscow on China and also deplored the Soviet intervention in Czechoslovakia. "The model of socialism for which we call on the Italian working class to struggle," he concluded, "is different from any other existing model."[3]

Over the following years Berlinguer developed a concept of co-existence within a pluralist society that was radically different from previous communist positions. In a series of articles published in September and October 1973 in *Rinascità*, an Italian communist journal, he proposed what he called "the historic compromise." Recalling the recent overthrow of President Allende in Chile by the army supported by transnational corporations and the CIA, he said that even if the Left obtained 51 percent of the votes in Italy, it still would be unable to govern. "The character of imperialism and especially of North American imperialism is still economic and political suffocation," he wrote. Insisting that this tendency of imperialism could be checked only by a change in the balance of forces within the peoples aspiring to liberation, he proposed, as the only way forward for Italy, "a new great historic compromise" that would create an unbeatable coalition of the vast majority of Italians, communists, socialists, and Catholics.[4]

Eurocommunism has become a force principally in the European countries of Catholic culture, and this has not been accidental. The sociocultural conditions for a rapprochement were particularly good in those countries after World War II. The confessional political parties that had long been a feature of Western Europe lost much of their significance in the postwar world, and Catholic workers began to join socialist parties in substantial numbers. In the 1960s, Vatican Council II inaugurated a new level of ecumenism which further reduced the importance of confessional parties.

Simultaneously in all Western Europe the parties of the Left gained a hitherto unknown prominence. By the mid-1970s, the Labour Party was back in power in Britain. The Social Democratic Party ruled in Bonn. The Socialist Party had won two elections in Sweden under Olaf Palme. Mario Soares was prime minister of post-fascist Portugal. The Spanish socialists were in the process of becoming the second party in a newly democratic Spain. In both France and Italy, the Socialist Party and the Communist Party between them garnered more than half the votes in national elections. Such electoral victories could only have occurred because very many who identified themselves as Christians had voted for parties of the Left.

The Italian Communist Party

In Italy, for example, the Communist Party received more votes in 1976 than ever before, 34.4 percent of the ballots, second only to the Christian Democrats with 38.7 percent. Several major cities, including Rome for the first time ever, elected Communist Party mayors. The Party seemed finally on the brink of power, and a public debate followed as to the likely effect on Italian society. Bishop Luigi Bettazzi of Ivrea wrote an open letter to Berlinguer as general secretary of the Party. The bishop expressed his support for a political program that would vigorously promote social justice and greater equality among all citizens. He expressed his belief that the Christians who had voted for the Communist Party, with no intention of abandoning their religious faith, had done so in the belief that they were promoting "a more just, more solid, more participatory, and therefore more Christian, society." He praised as "courageous" the Party's decision to include prominent Christians in their list of candidates in the recent elections.

Given this very novel situation of massive support by professed Christians, the bishop continued, he felt justified in asking a clear commitment that Catholics and Christians would not be discriminated against if the Communist Party actually came to power. The Party's stand, both domestic and international, he noted approvingly, "seems to aim at the realization of an original experience in communism, different from the communisms of other nations." Given this fact, the time seemed to have come to examine what changes might be desirable in policy and practice. "A more mature reflection, favored by the cultural and social experiences of thirty years of parliamentary democracy, might thus lead to an attitude which, without giving up anything in terms of concreteness and dynamism in social renewal, sets aside the superfluous ideological aspects and certain counterproductive methods in practical social action."

To be even more specific, the bishop concluded, "the greatest fear that many people feel in the face of your advance stems from foreign experiences. In too many countries, the legitimate effort for a socialist renewal of the collectivity is accompanied by violent excesses in the suppression of too many freedoms, including religious freedom, when human life itself is not actually jeopardized."[5]

In his reply, published in Rome in October 1977 during a synod attended by bishops from all parts of the world on the occasion of the eightieth birthday of Pope Paul VI, Berlinguer insisted on the "full and rigorous secularity" of the Italian Communist Party. He cited Clause 2 of its Statute, ratified in January 1946: "All citizens who have attained eighteen years of age and who — regardless of race, religious faith, and philosophical convictions — accept the Party's political program and pledge themselves to work to realize it, to observe the Statute and to work in a Party organization, may join the Italian Communist Party." On the basis of this Clause, Berlinguer continued, they had built "a new Party," neither sectarian nor integralist, a party that as a political organization does not profess explicitly the Marxist ideology "as a materialistic and atheistic philosophy."

What this means, Berlinguer explained, is that the Italian Party derives its inspiration from

the great and living lesson — which is not the same thing as an "ideological creed" — left to us by the masters of revolutionary political thinking, by the founders of the Communist movement. The discoveries and inventions of these masters constitute an invaluable patrimony, upon which not only our Party but the working-class and revolutionary movement in all parts of the world has drawn and continues to draw: a patrimony which has given life to a multiplicity of liberation movements and to a great variety of experiences in the construction of anticapitalist societies moving along the road to socialism. Without this patrimony, indeed, without a Marxist analysis — that is to say, without a Marxism understood and used critically as a lesson, not accepted and read dogmatically as an unchangeable text — the positions the Italian Communist Party holds today, and even the growth of its organizational and electoral strength, would be completely unexplainable.

Given this context, Berlinguer added,

I think the positions the Italian Communist Party has adopted and its conduct over the course of some decades should be sufficient to convince you that taken together they form a valid guarantee that it is not only determined to build here in Italy a Party that is secular and democratic and, as such, neither theist nor atheist nor antitheist, but also, as a direct consequence, desires a secular, democratic state that is likewise neither theist nor atheist nor antitheist.

The Party's fifteenth national congress in 1979 continued the same line. Having reaffirmed the principle of respect for religion and its commitment to religious freedoms, it added: "The Italian Communist Party, as such, does not profess atheism.... It hopes for an understanding with those Catholic movements and forces in which are found operative tendencies and demands for social, civil, and moral renewal."

The Fifteenth Congress also made a remarkable clarification of the Party's position on an important issue of Marxist theory. "Sensitive to the reality of the religious dimension," it said, "Italian communists have gone beyond the notion that increased scientific knowledge and changed social structures would suffice to effect radical change as regards ways of thinking and human conscience."[6]

What this implies is the rejection of a simplistic Marxism which saw religion as simply the result of economic relations and thus automatically eliminated by changing the economic system. That attitude resulted from the acceptance of a mechanistic determinism in human affairs, in the relation between infrastructure and superstructure as formulated by Marx, between social existence and conscience. A certain autonomy of the sphere of religion is recognized. By refusing to make an ideological, philosophical, or metaphysical judgment on the religious phenomenon, the Party implicitly recognizes the possibility of the experience of faith even within a socialist or communist society.

Centrifugal Forces

Similar positions have been adopted by the Spanish Communist Party and the Catalan United Socialist Party (also communist). Their official documents insist on the laicity of the Communist

Party and also of Marxism and recognize a relative autonomy of the religious experience as found in many different historical expressions. Typical is an October 1977 Catalan statement that certain forms of atheism, in the same way as certain forms of religiosity, "serve only to prevent personal and collective emancipation." It calls for an organized effort to insist, in both praxis and theory, on separating atheism and communism, and atheism and Marxism.

Approaching the issue, not from an ideological, but from a historical starting point, the statement offers an analysis that takes into account the diversity of positions within the Catholic church.

Our Party will have to keep criticizing the church as an instrument of state ideology in the present and future situations, as shown by the Vatican's connections with imperialism and multinational enterprises, as well as its political maneuvers in Europe aimed at maintaining a moderate policy which — through a formal acceptance of human rights — will perpetuate the ideological supremacy of a conservative hierarchy and the survival of the capitalist system. At the same time, the Party's analysis must consider the constantly increasing number of believers, all over the world, who firmly fight against imperialism, thus demonstrating the fallacy of those who consider Christianity as a whole to be a direct consequence of capitalist relations of production....

It is now necessary to overcome the traditional identification of the Communist option with atheism, owing to the shortcomings of the Marxist criticism of religion in adapting to the present historical moment. Marxism was born of atheism as an expression of the ideological struggles of those times. But if we believe that Marxism is, above all, a dialectical method which, in conjunction with a class practice, allows us to analyze and change society, we should ask ourselves whether atheism is a basic element of the Marxist method and, especially, whether it should be considered a necessity in a Communist society. We will continue to have atheist Communists who will fight in the common struggle for socialism together with Christian Communists and others of different philosophical beliefs, with the same civil rights, avoiding the attitude that these beliefs belong exclusively to the "private sphere." On the contrary, encouragement should be given to overcome the privatization of the religious and philosophical conscience of activists through open debate among the different cultural currents present in the Party.[7]

Following the death of General Franco in November 1975, the long proscribed Spanish Communist Party emerged as a major political force under the leadership of Santiago Carrillo, who quickly established himself as a critic of the Soviet system's "distortions" of Marxism. He publicly proclaimed the autonomy of the Spanish Party at a meeting in Berlin in 1976 of the Pan-European Conference of Communist Parties. The militant Marxists of the early twentieth century, he said, were like the early Christians. As Rome for the Christians, so Moscow for them was the ruler of a new Marxist Church. "Those were the days of our infancy. Now we are grown up. We communists have no leading center, no international discipline which can be forced upon us. What unites us are bonds of affinity. . . . We accept no return to the structures and concepts of an internationalism of former times."[8]

The French Communist Party has been more guarded in its criticism of Moscow. It has, nevertheless, indicated its basic identification with the other parties of Western Europe, most specifically in a joint statement with the Italian Party in November 1975 which "reconfirmed the principle of the autonomy of each party, of respect, noninterference, and internationalism." In the process of creating a socialist society, they say,

all the freedoms — which are a product both of the great democratic-bourgeois revolutions and of the great popular struggles of this century headed by the working class — will have to be guaranteed and developed. This holds true for freedom of thought and expression, for freedom of the press, of assembly, association, and demonstration, for free movement of persons inside and outside their country, for the inviolability of private life, for religious freedom and total freedom of expression for currents of thought and every philosophical, cultural, and artistic opinion. The French and Italian communists declare themselves for the plurality of parties, for the right to existence and activity of opposition parties, for the free formation of majorities and minorities and the possibility of their alternating democratically.[9]

During the preparations for the Conference of European Communist Parties, held in Berlin in July 1976, the Italian, Spanish, and French Parties not only acted in concert but seemed to be seeking a formal relationship with other communist parties outside the Soviet sphere of influence. A meeting of the Italian Party with the Japanese Party in Tokyo in 1975 bore fruit in another meeting in Rome in 1977 at which the Japanese adopted the essentials of Eurocommunism. During that period, also, the Communist Party of India adopted a similar line, and the British Communist Party accepted many of the positions of the Eurocommunists, while continuing its resistance to the European Economic Community.[10]

It is significant that Moscow, while frequently expressing its disapproval of these centrifugal movements in communism, has not attempted excommunication or other actions calculated to force an open break, as it always did to dissidence in the past. Even Rumania, within its immediate sphere of influence, made common cause with the Western European Parties without a repetition of the strong-arm methods used against Hungary in 1956 or Czechoslovakia in 1968. One may see a parallel in the gradual dissolution of the British Empire, with recognition at the Imperial Conference of 1926 of the de facto independence of the members of what had then begun to call itself the Commonwealth, and the subsequent withering away of ties until little more remains than what Carrillo has well described as "bonds of affinity."

The Encounters

In parallel with these developments in Western European communism, dialogue developed both in Europe and in North America between spokespersons for both sides seeking to identify points of agreement and the possible further refinement of divisive issues. Outstanding among the pioneers was Ernst Bloch (1885–1977). As professor of philosophy at Leipzig in East Germany in the 1950s, he argued that Marxism, correctly understood, was a method of analysis requiring perpetual renewal. It could not be reconciled, he insisted, with the dictatorship of the proletariat, neglect of democracy, freedom, and respect for the law.[11] Under heavy criticism from the regime, Bloch moved in 1961 to Tübingen in West Germany, where he finally published his most famous work, *The Principle of Hope*, written a quarter of a century earlier while he was a refugee in the United States from Hitler's Germany.

This book helped to rehabilitate the notion of utopia, which had been given an extremely negative connotation by Engels and other Marxists. Bloch's message is summed up in the following lyrical statement:

There is a spirit of utopia in the final predicate of every great statement, in Strasbourg cathedral and in the Divine Comedy, in the expectant music of Beethoven and in the latencies of the Mass in B minor. It is in the despair which still contains an unum necessarium even as something is lost, and in the Hymn to Joy. Kyrie and Credo rise in the concept of utopia as that of comprehended hope in a completely different way, even when the reflection of mere time-bound ideology has been shed, precisely then. The exact imagination of the Not-Yet-Conscious thus completes the critical enlightenment itself, by revealing the gold that was not affected by aqua fortis [nitric acid], and the good content which remains most valid, indeed rises when class illusion, class ideology have been destroyed. Thus beyond the end of class ideologies, for which it could only be mere decoration up till then, culture has no other loss than the business of decoration itself, of falsely concluding harmonization. Utopian function tears the concerns of human culture away from such an idle bed of mere contemplation: it thus opens up, on truly attained summits, the ideologically unobstructed view of the content of human hope.[12]

Bloch greatly influenced Jürgen Moltmann, who as a fellow professor at Tübingen became his close friend. "Ever seeking for justice and freedom and ever disappointed anew," Moltmann has written of Bloch, "he sets before us a secular hope which has been sustained through many sufferings. He is a Marxist with a Bible in his hand, a Marxist who has hoped for greater things than socialism is able to fabricate."[13] Developing Bloch's theme, Moltmann concluded *The Theology of Hope* with an appeal to Christians to throw themselves unreservedly into the task of further perfecting creation.

The hope of resurrection must bring about a new understanding of the world. This world is not the heaven of self-realization, as it was said to be in Idealism. This world is not the hell of self-estrangement, as it is said to be in romanticist and existentialist writing. The world is not yet finished, but is understood as engaged in a history. It is therefore the world of possibilities, the world in which we can serve the future, promised truth and righteousness and peace. This is an age of diaspora, of sowing in hope, of self-surrender and sacrifice, for it is an age which stands within the horizon of a new future. Thus self-expenditure in this world, day-to-day love in hope, becomes possible and becomes human within that horizon of expectation which transcends this world. The glory of self-realization and the misery of self-estrangement alike arise from hopelessness in a world of lost horizons. To disclose to it the horizon of the future of the crucified Christ is the task of the Christian church.[14]

Through Moltmann, Bloch also influenced liberation theologian Rubem Alves, author of *A Theology of Human Hope*, and other liberation theologians.

In 1965, a group of German-speaking theologians and scientists created the Paulusgesellschaft, the first public and international attempt at a Christian-Marxist dialogue. Both Catholics and Protestants participated in two meetings with Marxists at Salzburg (Austria) and at Chiemsee, or Herrenchiemsee (Bavaria). They included Giulio Girardi, then professor of theoretical philosophy at the Salesian Atheneum in Rome, a consultant on atheism and nonbelievers during Vatican Council II.

Influenced by these meetings, Milan Machovec, a Marxist theoretician and professor at the University of Prague, organized the first Christian-Marxist encounter in Eastern Europe, at Marianske Lazne, better known by its former name of Marienbad (Czechoslovakia), in 1967. Participants included French Marxist theoretician Roger Garaudy, who spoke of a "latent atheism in Christianity that prevented it from serving false gods," Giulio Girardi, and Johannes Baptist Metz, who declared that Christian love could command even revolutionary violence. Metz, professor of fundamental theology at the University of Münster, West Germany, had been an important influence as a theological adviser at Vatican Council II. Marxists included Vitezslav Gardavsky, who said that Christians and Marxists should be able to trust each other to bear responsibility for the future of mankind, or as Christians would put it, "to work for the coming of God's kingdom"; and Milan Pruha, who pleaded for a pluralism in Marxism, and who said that Marxists should encourage Christians "to be even more radical in their striving for transcendence."[15]

The Paulusgesellschaft initiative helped to create what became known as the New Left, a movement that urged the church to cooperate more fully with secular organizations and political groupings, including socialists and communists.[16] And in 1965 Roger Garaudy had published *From Anathema to Dialogue*, with an Introduction by Jesuit Karl Rahner and an Epilogue by Johannes Baptist Metz. The Marxist dialectic, Garaudy wrote,

bears within itself the extraordinary Christian heritage [of transcendence], which it must investigate still more. Living Marxism, which has proved its fruitfulness and its effectiveness in history, in political economy, in revolutionary struggle, and in the building of socialism, owes it to itself in philosophy to work out a more profound theory of subjectivity, one which is not subjectivist, and a more profound theory of transcendence, one which is not alienated. In this investigation we can learn a great deal from Christianity.[17]

Rahner, for his part, developed his concept of God as the absolute future, so that a person who "makes himself open to his absolute future also experiences what is really meant by the word 'God'; and it is of secondary importance whether he uses the word or not, whether or not he explicitly reflects on this unity of absolute future and God."[18]

Pursuing the same theme, Metz refers to the account of the revelation of God in Exodus 3:14:

Certainly God is said there to be our future, but *our* future in so far as this future belongs to itself, is grounded in itself, and is not simply the correlative of our wishes and strivings: "I will be who I will be," runs the central phrase of the passage mentioned. It defines the deity of God as free, self-belonging dynamism of our future and not primarily as "Being above us," in the sense of a beyond that is to be experienced outside history.[19]

Also in the mid-sixties, influential Catholics, including Paulo Freire, Giulio Girardi, and Ivan Illich, and groups like Frères du Monde in France and Slant in England opted for what they called Marxism with a human face. The Slant group identified itself as moving beyond dialogue to collaboration. In its view, an intellectual synthesis of Christianity and Marxism, even if it could be achieved, would be inadequate; there should be a form of life in which people would have integrated and could live out both traditions.

In 1974, at a further meeting of the Paulusgesellschaft, in Vienna, German theologian Dorothee Sölle, a professor at Union Theological Seminary, New York, described in a striking self-analysis the processes by which a Christian theologian makes the option for socialism.

A new specter is racing through the parishes and offices of the church, its synods and theology schools, its study circles and communication media — the specter of a Christian opting for socialism. For a long time, the message of Jesus could only be encountered in a canalized form — domesticated by scientific exercises and historical-cultural considerations opposed to any action, limited to small church-related groups which became more and more marginal in relation to society as a whole, and at the service of a quasi-automatic and unconscious identification of Christian behavior with social conformism. But against all expectation, even on the part of those who believe in progress, the message drives those who identify with it beyond themselves, it exiles them, making them guilty of criminality — as recently became clear in the campaign led against Kurt Scharf, the Evangelical Bishop of Berlin, because of his visit to the prisoners known as the Baader Meinhof gang. It destroys a tacit agreement with the permanent injustice of society. It makes impossible what is asked of us each day — the submission of all human desires and needs to the imperatives of a system of production and consumption.... This [new] identity is born of the experience of class struggle and of a faith that has been lived; for an increasing number of men and women these two experiences can no longer be separated from each other because they are reciprocally conditioned, nourish each other, and are expressing and organizing themselves in a new language. We are Christians and at the same time socialists; it has become impossible to define ourselves by the simple designation, "I am Christian," because that expression allows for too many misunderstandings and tends rather to obscure the fact of being Christian "for the kingdom of God."[20]

In April 1969, a two-day conference on "Marxism, Religion, and the Liberal Tradition" was held in the United States at Temple University, Philadelphia. Herbert Marcuse, the principal Marxist theoretician at the conference, concluded that Marxian theory remains irreconcilable with Christian dogma and its institutions but

Marxism finds an ally "in those tendencies, groups, and individuals committed to the part of the Christian teaching that stands uncompromisingly against inhuman, exploitative power." At the same time he recognized that "something in the basic Marxian conception itself...seems to continue repressive tendencies and extend them from the old societies to the new." This is important as an admission of the need for reform and the incompleteness of the Marxist worldview. And while the Marcuse admissions run counter to the practice of Soviet Marxists who until recently laid claim to a privileged access to truth, by virtue of their "scientific" system, they are fully consonant with Marx's insistence that his system is scientific and consequently subject to verification and correction in accordance with the scientific method.

The Soviet invasion of Czechoslovakia in the previous year had an impact on the Christian-Marxist dialogue in two contradictory ways. It renewed suspicions in the West about the possibility of ever being able to trust communists. Simultaneously, however, it pushed many Western Marxists further away from the Marxist-Leninist line which the Soviets then claimed to be the exclusive orthodox kind of Marxism, thereby increasing their emotional willingness to look for ways to permit better relations with Christians. Meanwhile, during the 1970s there was a significant growth in conservatism in the United States, Britain, West Germany, and generally in industrialized Western countries, a conservatism that carried with it a revival of the Cold War militant anticommunism. Pope John Paul II, elected in 1978, has reestablished practices and seeks to establish attitudes that would reverse much of the momentum of Vatican Council II. Such an atmosphere inhibits both Catholics and Marxists who seek to identify their differences and search for mutually acceptable solutions, or who even want to cooperate in the pursuit of common objectives. The pope's meeting with President Gorbachev in 1989, however, as mentioned earlier, holds promise of a significant reversal of this negative trend.

Latin American Dialogue

The decrease in dialogue in Europe has not affected Latin America. In this area of predominantly Christian tradition, the issue of collaboration with communists was always formulated in very different terms. Dialogue has never been to any significant extent in the form of conferences of specialists, but rather at the level of praxis, of common commitment to the revolutionary change of a society agreed by both sides to be irreformable.

Referring to the dialogue in Europe, Roger Garaudy has described it as not an end in itself but as a way to concrete cooperation in confronting the crucial problems of our times, war and social revolution.[21] But in Latin America, as José Míguez Bonino points out:

The order seems to be reversed: cooperation leads to dialogue.... The European "dialogue" frequently begins with "two systems of truth," two self-contained and self-sufficient conceptual entities, almost two ideologies which confront each other, compare their views and derive from them certain practical conclusions on the basis of which cooperation is either possible or excluded. In the Latin American situation, on the other hand, we are faced with men who are engaged in certain forms of action in relation to given conditions. These courses of action are, to be sure, related to theoretical views and horizons of meaning. But it is not as conceptual vision but as historical practice that they come into contact, opposition, or cooperation. Consequently, the theoretical discussion — the "dialogue" in the European sense of the word — arises as the explication, background, and projection of this practice.

The underlying reason, says Míguez, quoting Julio de Santa Ana, is that in Latin America "the circumstances that condition the situation of individuals, not communist ideology, constitute the true challenge to the church."[22]

In Latin America, in addition, even though there is a lay — at times, atheistic — tradition in influential intellectual circles, atheism is nowhere a mass phenomenon. Theoretical discussion is consequently carried on largely, not between Christians and Marxists, but as part of the political encounter of Christian conservatives and progressives. When the former denounce Marxism as atheistic, the others reply that the real atheists are the conservatives themselves. The progressives borrow the notion of fetishism developed by Marx in *Capital*. The fetishism of products, of money, of capital, is a false representation, an idol, resulting from mercantile relations. Capitalism is consequently a false religion, the religion denounced by Marx. Christianity is the religion that repudiates false idols. These are issues that concern the theology of liberation, the subject of the next chapter.

Chapter 6

Theology of Liberation

As the Christians for Socialism movement spread, it was buttressed by the parallel development of a radically new theology that was definitively given its name by a Peruvian Indian, Gustavo Gutiérrez, when in 1971 he published *A Theology of Liberation*. Gutiérrez, who had studied in Europe and taught theology at the Catholic University of Peru, first used the expression "theology of liberation" at a meeting at Chimbote, Peru, in July 1968.[1] Also in 1971, Hugo Assmann, a Brazilian, published what has also become a classic of the theology of liberation, *Theology for a Nomad Church*. Leonardo Boff, also a Brazilian, followed them in 1972 with *Jesus Christ Liberator*. The originality of this theology was threefold. It was the first Christian theology ever developed in Latin America. Instead of adopting philosophy as its starting point, it used sociology as source of its reflection. And it insists on the preferential option for the poor as its central focus, an option that demands that the Christian message be formulated in terms that promote the liberation of the oppressed masses.

The development of this first Latin American Christian theology can be traced through several phases. A preparatory phase stretches from 1962 to 1968, that is to say, from the beginning of Vatican Council II — which institutionalized Pope John XXIII's *aggiornamento* — to the application of the Council to the conditions of Latin America and its reinterpretation in the light of those conditions by the second conference of the Latin American bishops at

79

Medellín, Colombia. Although Medellín never used the technical expression "theology of liberation," it made wide use of liberation as a category.

Next came a formative phase in which the specific approach and the central content became available in the books mentioned above and others. This continued to 1975, the year in which Latin American theologians made contact at the Theology in the Americas conference (Detroit, U.S.A,) with a very different context: black theology, feminist theology, the theological and social realities of Native Americans, Chicanos, Puerto Ricans, Asian Americans, working-class people, the Appalachian poor, evangelical radicalism, and more traditional Catholic and Protestant schools of "liberal" theology. After that event, they began to speak of liberation theologies in the plural. The systematizing phase that followed has been engaged in reflecting on methods and in the systematic rethinking of the main themes of theology, especially christology and ecclesiology.[2]

A Latin American Theology

In Latin America, as elsewhere in the Third World, all theology had been imported from Europe. Its concerns were the concerns of Europe. Taking sociology as the basis for reflection, the theologians of liberation began by looking at their specific existential situation. While European theologians in the fourth quarter of the twentieth century might be agitated about the "death of God" or papal infallibility, one who looked at Latin America could not but give priority to the moral issues raised by starving people and the institutionalization of death squads to maintain order without justice.

"Commitment to the process of liberation in Latin America," to quote Assmann,

means starting from a particular analysis of our situation as oppressed peoples, [and] opting for a particular social analysis is not a neutral step. It involves the necessary choice of an ethical and political stance; there is no such thing as an uninvolved social science, and to pretend that there is is itself to adopt a reactionary ideological position. This fact has already become central to discussions of methodology on the level of the social sciences. There is probably no more obvious example of a committed science anywhere today than sociology in Latin America, which has taken the decisive step of making "dependence" the central theme of its investigations into the real situation in Latin America. The situation of dependence is the basic starting-point for the process of liberation. On the theological level an analysis of dependence has produced the language of the theology of liberation.[3]

The theological breakthrough followed, and could not have happened without, a breakthrough at the level of the human sciences. Argentine economist Raúl Prebisch had told the first meeting of the United Nations Commission on Trade and Development (UNCTAD) in 1964 that the "periphery" must consistently sell its raw materials for less while the manufacturing products of the "center" are sold for consistently higher prices, a structural and growing disequilibrium. This was the repudiation of the Alliance for Progress theory of developmentalism for a theory of dependence which proclaimed that the poverty of the peripheral countries is the result of systematic exploitation by the countries of the center. Modified versions of the dependency theory have been formulated by other economists who seek to explain the significant economic growth of such countries as Brazil, South Korea, and Taiwan. Such development, they say, remains dependent and may even increase dependency, because it means the control of key industrial sectors by foreign firms, the introduction of inappropriate technology, and increased maldistribution of the national income. Without becoming involved in the technical discussion, the theologians of liberation find the general concept of dependency valuable in their analysis of the reality of the Third World and a starting point for their theological reflection.[4]

In parallel with the Catholics, Gutiérrez and Assmann, Protestant theologians Rubem Alves and Richard Shaull were in the late 1960s discussing the desirability of moving from a theology of development or a theology of hope to a theology of liberation. In 1966, at a meeting of Church and Society in Geneva, Shaull raised the issue of the relationship between the Christian vocation and the participation of Christians in the revolutionary struggle. While not proposing the development of a systematic theology of revolution, Shaull thought that the Christian vocation could nourish an authentic revolutionary vocation. In the ensuing debate Helmut Gollwitzer and Jürgen Moltmann, both European theologians, offered an eschatological framework for revolution, the apocalyptic break with the past that ushers in the reign of God. As Moltmann expressed it, the symbols and the images of the Bible stress the discontinuity, the condemnation, the end of the world, and the outbreak of something completely new.[5]

The theology of liberation immediately sought to differentiate itself from this European approach, an approach Hugo Assmann criticized as abstract, not grounded in a concrete existential situation. In the language of the theology of liberation, it was not reflection as "a second act." Gustavo Gutiérrez, in a more general distancing of the theology of liberation from all "progressive" European theologies, accuses them of not bringing into the discussion the concrete historical basis on which the modern world is fashioned.[6]

The theologians of liberation were agreed from the outset that a proper understanding of their faith and the obligations it imposes requires Christians to make a correct analysis of their concrete historical situation. They rejected the European approach to theology by deductive reasoning from abstract first principles in favor of a praxis, a frame of action derived from observation and analysis of facts and of one's own reality. This, they argued, requires a mainly economic analysis of the oppression of the poor majority of Latin Americans. Social analysis is consequently for them the first step toward theology. In the expression of Gutiérrez, theology is never *actus primus* ("first act or movement"); it is always *actus secundus* ("second act"). It is the reflection on the struggle for emancipation.

One of the remarkable things about this first truly Latin American theology is that it involved from the outset Catholic and Protestant theologians working in close cooperation. The Catholics Assmann, Gutiérrez, José Porfirio Miranda, Juan Luis Segundo, Jon Sobrino, Paul Blanquart, Noel Olaya, and J. Severino Croatto are matched by the Protestants Alves, Shaull, Julio Barreiro, José Míguez Bonino, Julio de Santa Ana, Emilio Castro, and Elsa Tamez. Yet perhaps this transcending of the sixteenth-century Reformation is not so strange. The Reformation was a European phenomenon, historically conditioned by economic, political, and cultural differences in that continent. It was imposed on Latin America as an integral part of the European colonization of the hemisphere. Latin American Christians had to transcend it as one step in liberating themselves.

Marxism

Most theologians of liberation use Marxist analysis as an analytic tool, and its use is at least implicit in the theory of dependence. This theory rests on the general methodological assumption that there exist relatively enduring social structures that limit the range of possibilities at a given historical moment. It is properly described as neo-Marxist, not formulated by Marx himself but a product of the research tradition whose initial, paradigmatic exemplar is Marx's *Capital*.

Much of the criticism of the theology of liberation has centered on its use of the Marxist analysis. It should be noted, however, that it had slipped into Catholic thinking, as into the entire contemporary culture, in many ways before Gutiérrez and his associates. Pius XI in *Quadragesimo Anno* reflects the essential elements both of the analysis and of the Marxist critique of capitalism, and his lead has been followed in all subsequent papal documents dealing with the social order. Pope John Paul II's *Laborem Exercens* owes even more to Marx than any previous papal pronouncement, especially the insistence on the central role of work. But borrowings from Marxism by no means constitute the central novelty or contribution of the theology of liberation. In its evaluation of this theology, the Theology Center of Kerala, India, has commented that

the revolutionary thing about this theology is not any alleged Marxist content but the miracle of the Good News coming alive for the oppressed, of theology grounding itself, among other things, in the experience of the poor and speaking to them, and of their wanting to grow as a community that is more loyal to the church even as they try to respond to the demands of their human dignity.[7]

Cardinal Josef Ratzinger, head of the Congregation for the Doctrine of the Faith (successor to the Holy Office and to the

Inquisition), does not, however, view Marxism as peripheral to the theology of liberation. He believes, on the contrary, that this theology is so infected by Marxist ideology as to be incompatible with Christian belief. In his *Instruction on Certain Aspects of the "Theology of Liberation"* (1984), Cardinal Ratzinger asserts that it is impossible to separate the analysis from the other elements of Marxism. "The thought of Marx is such a global vision of reality that all data received from observation and analysis are brought together in a philosophical and ideological structure which predetermines the significance and importance to be attached to them. The ideological principles come prior to the study of the social reality and are presupposed in it. Thus no separation of the parts of this epistemologically unique complex is possible. If one tries to take only one part, say, the analysis, one ends up having to accept the entire ideology."[8]

Jesuit theologian Juan Luis Segundo refutes this argument at length. It is enough to quote a short passage. Having noted that the theologians of liberation he knows only take elements of the Marxist analysis and "complement and correct" these elements from other sources, he adds:

If they [the elements of analysis] were impossible to separate from the rest of Marxist thought, how is it that well-known non-Marxist and even anti-Marxist thinkers and sociologists — such as Weber or Mannheim — can use these analytical tools without being pushed to the same consequences? The Supreme Pontiff himself [Pope John Paul II] makes excellent use of Marxist analysis, such as the category of *alienation*, to describe the worker who gives up the fruits of his or her labor in exchange for a salary in capitalist (or socialist) countries.[9]

Other commentators agree with Segundo's criticism of Ratzinger's claim that the elements of Marxism are inseparable. "It is one thing, however," writes Anselm K. Min,

to say something is necessarily related to other parts *within* a particular system, and quite another to say that it is so inseparable from that system that its meaning is exhausted by its place within that system. The meaning a concept actually possesses within a system need not be the only meaning it may have, unless that system is so comprehensive and so penetrating as to exhaust all reality without remainder. Even Hegel's system did not claim such perfection. The meaning of a concept may transcend its particular embodiment within a given system, just as a different system or a new context may disclose a new meaning of the concept not present in the old. A concept and a context can enrich and transform each other in a positive dialectic, just as they can impoverish and corrupt each other in a negative. In neither case is a concept inseparable from its old context and meaning and its meaning exhausted by it. In a real sense the whole history of philosophy is a history in which parts of a system get separated from their old matrix and emigrate to a new home, a new system with which they enter into a dialectical relationship.

John Paul himself, I think, is a good example of this dialectic. He takes the concept of "person" in Boethius, Thomas, Kant, Scheler, and others, criticizes it, and transforms its meaning with his own interpretation in *The Acting Person*. He also takes terms and ideas, undoubtedly Marxian in origin, such as "labor," "social leader," "alienation," "transformation of nature," "proletarianization," "social subject," "opposition between capital and labor," and others, and "personalizes" their meaning.[10]

Gregory Baum pursues the same line of thought. Stressing the dialectic of transformative appropriation in *Laborem Exercens*, he comments:

While the encyclical remains in continuity with the Church's social teaching, it introduces new ideas, derived from a critical and creative dialogue with Marxism, which allow the author to reread the Catholic tradition in a new light.... Yet in the discussion of these insights he opens them up, and thus produces a social philosophy which transcends Marxism from within.[11]

The International Theological Commission created by Paul VI set up a committee in 1974 to study the theology of liberation. Its report, as approved at a meeting of the Commission in Rome in October 1976, commented as follows on the issue of Marxist analysis by theologians:

The prophetic accusations of injustice and the call for solidarity with the poor refer to very complex, historically developed, and socio-politically determined issues. Even a prophetic judgment of the time [kairos] requires criteria. In consequence, the different theological explorations of liberation necessarily employ sociological theories that try to analyze the "Cry of the People" calmly and objectively. Theology cannot deduce concrete political rules of conduct from theological principles alone. The theologian cannot, therefore, simply with his own resources, resolve basic sociological conflicts. Theological explorations seeking to create a more human society must keep in mind the related dangers when dealing with sociological theories. These must be scrutinized continuously to determine their level of credibility. Often they are mere hypotheses, which not infrequently contain explicit or implicit ideological elements based on controversial philosophical assumptions or on a wrong understanding of human nature. This holds good, for example, of important parts of Marxist-Leninist oriented social analyses. When dealing with such theories and analyses one must be careful not to give them a higher level of credibility because theology has incorporated them into its discussions. At the same time, theology must recognize a plurality of scholarly interpretations and must not commit itself to one concrete sociological analysis based on any kind of necessity.[12]

The liberation theologians make class analysis the central and indisputable element for understanding the social situation, and they stress the major impact on political and cultural developments of the interests of the class that owns and controls the major means of production. They similarly repeat Marx's critique of the fetishism of capitalism. And they are emotionally close to Marx's "materialism" in their insistence that salvation is not just a matter of an afterlife but is the proper goal of all human endeavor on earth.

All of them, however, reject Marx's atheism which, following the lead of various Eurocommunists, they insist is not an integral part of his system. But with the sole exception of José Porfirio Miranda, Mexican author of a work of biblical exegesis, *Marx and the Bible*, and a philosophical polemic, *Marx Against the Marxists*, they have not devoted systematic attention to Marxism. Their widespread use of Marxist terminology and concepts simply reflects the fact that Marx has become as much a part of the intellectual context in Latin America as Freud is in the United States.

Backlash

The 1960s were marked with euphoria in both church and state. There was a sense that everything was possible, that we had reached a level that provided both the ability and the will to renew the face of the earth. Although the theologians of liberation rejected this easy optimism, they benefited for a time from its existence. As early as 1966, Archbishop Helder Camara of Recife, Brazil, and sixteen other Third World bishops declared that "the people of the Third World constitute the proletariat of the present world." And in 1971, Archbishop (later Cardinal) Eduardo Pironio of Argentina, then secretary general of the regional council of the Latin American bishops, CELAM, declared that "our mission, like Christ's, consists of bringing the good news to the poor, of proclaiming liberation to the oppressed."[13]

The honeymoon, however, didn't last long. Almost all of Latin America experienced military dictatorships which quickly identified the theology of liberation as a major challenge to their doctrine of National Security. Many liberation theologians were driven into exile. Others had difficulty in publishing their work. In addition, both Catholic and Protestant churches experienced reaction. Rubem Alves could not publish in Brazil for many years and he found himself in such conflict with the Presbyterian denomination in which he had been ordained that he withdrew from it.

The reactionary mood expressed itself in the Catholic church also when in 1972 the bishops of Latin America chose Bishop (now Cardinal) Alfonso López Trujillo as secretary general of CELAM. López concentrated CELAM's training institutes under his personal supervision in Bogotá, Colombia; and together with Belgian Jesuit Roger Vekemans, who the previous year had fled Allende's Chile and established a base in Colombia, he began a war to the death on the theology of liberation. This theology, according to Vekemans, supports the Marxist-Leninist model of revolution and is in fact a theology of revolution. It even advocates revolution in the church, "contesting her hierarchical authority and reducing her teaching power to mere circumstantial writings, which are qualified as obsolete, if not counterrevolutionary."[14]

Many of the Latin American bishops shared the reservations of López Trujillo and Vekemans. A few nevertheless continued to defend the new approach, one of the most outspoken being Archbishop Helder Camara. In a talk at the University of Chicago in 1974, he recalled that Thomas Aquinas had been attacked from all sides for presuming to use Aristotle as the starting point for his theology. Aristotle, Helder Camara said, was then regarded as a pagan, a materialist, a dangerous person, a sinner.

One might ask what a Christian thinker could possibly learn from Aristotle, whose basic position contradicted essential points of Christian teaching.... The Aristotelian system was so monolithic that it must have seemed impossible to accept some of its truths without accepting the entire system.... Even more admirable than [Aquinas's] courage was his lifelong quest for truth. Searching for truth, no matter how hidden, no matter how distorted, imprisoned, or apparently demented, Thomas did not stint his efforts or refuse any sacrifices.

The parallel with the current situation, in Helder Camara's view, is remarkable:

Marx... challenges our courage because he is a materialist, a militant atheist, an agitator, a subversive, an anti-Christian. Yet he too has in his system (why deny it?) certain truths that undoubtedly advance the development of human thought.... Perhaps the best way to honor [Thomas Aquinas] would be to try to do today with Karl Marx what Saint Thomas did in his day with Aristotle.[15]

Puebla

The Latin American bishops decided to hold a third General Conference (CELAM III) at Puebla, Mexico, in late 1978, a decade after the Medellín meeting. López Trujillo decided to use this opportunity to obtain a formal condemnation of the use of Marxist elements by the theologians, similar to the condemnation of the Aristotelianism of Aquinas by the Archbishop of Paris (the city at whose university Aquinas had taught) seven centuries earlier. As head of the bishops' secretariat charged with preparing the conference agenda, he was able to exclude from the process the progressive theologians who had played a decisive part in drafting the documents for the Medellín meeting. The documents drawn up in complete secrecy under his supervision incorporated his evaluation of the theology of liberation as not consonant with Christian faith. To ensure their passage, he lobbied at the Vatican to prevent the selection of some potential delegates, the best known of whom was Jesuit superior general Pedro Arrupe.

While the documents were being printed, however, the text was leaked, and a pirated edition was widely circulated before the delegates received their numbered copies. Distinguished theologians in several countries led the chorus of protest at the distortions contained in the draft documents and at the attempt to manipulate the meeting. The deaths in quick succession of Pope Paul VI and Pope John Paul I in the fall of 1978 caused the meeting to be postponed until late January 1979, allowing further time for the theologians of liberation to organize their defense. Although still excluded from the meeting, they were present in Puebla and were able to provide significant input. Father Arrupe participated as a delegate named by Pope John Paul II.[16]

An intense struggle at the meeting produced this text:

Some believe it is possible to separate various aspects of Marxism — its doctrine and its method of analysis in particular. But we would remind people of the teaching of the papal magisterium on this point. "It would be illusory and dangerous to reach a point of forgetting the intimate link that radically binds them [the ideology and the analysis] together; to accept the elements of Marxist analysis without recognizing their relationships with ideology, and to enter into the practice of the class struggle and its Marxist interpretations while failing to note the kind of totalitarian and violent society to which this process leads [*Octogesima Adveniens*, par. 34].

We must note the risk of ideologization run by theological reflection when it is based on a praxis that has recourse to Marxist analysis. The consequences are the total politicization of Christian existence, the disintegration of the language of faith into that of the social sciences, and the draining away of the transcendental dimensions of Christian salvation.[17]

The quotation from the teaching of the papal magisterium is from *Octogesima Adveniens*, Paul VI's 1971 letter commemorating the eightieth anniversary of *Rerum Novarum*, and addressed to Cardinal Roy of Quebec, then president of the Vatican's Justice and Peace Commission. The preceding sentences, which provide the necessary context, read:

For some, Marxism remains essentially the active practice of class struggle. Experiencing the ever present and continually renewed force of the relationships of domination and exploitation among men, they reduce Marxism to no more than a struggle — at times with no other purpose — to be pursued and even stirred up in permanent fashion. For others, it is first and foremost the collective exercise of political and economic power under the direction of a single party, which would be the sole expression and guarantee of the welfare of all, and would deprive individuals and other groups of any possibility of initiative and choice. At a third level, Marxism, whether in power or not, is viewed as a socialist ideology based on historical materialism and the denial of everything transcendent. At other times, finally, it presents itself in a more attenuated form, one also more attractive to the modern mind: as a scientific activity, as a rigorous method of examining social and theoretical knowledge, and as the rational link, tested by history, between theoretical knowledge and the practice of revolutionary transformation. Although this type of analysis gives a privileged position to certain aspects of reality to the detriment of the rest, and interprets them in the light of its ideology, it nevertheless furnishes some people not only with a working tool but also a certitude preliminary to action: the claim to decipher in a scientific manner the mainsprings of the evolution of society.

While, through the concrete existing form of Marxism, one can distinguish these various aspects and the questions they pose for the reflection and activity of Christians, it would be illusory and dangerous to reach a point of forgetting the intimate link which radically binds them together, to accept the elements of Marxist analysis without recognizing their relationships with ideology, and to enter into the practice of class struggle and its Marxist interpretations, while failing to note the kind of totalitarian and violent society to which this process leads.[18]

In this historic passage, Paul VI was changing papal teaching on Marxism radically. Previously it was accorded only anathemas. "Socialism, if it remains truly socialism," Pius XI had written in *Quadragesimo Anno*, "cannot be reconciled with the teachings of the Catholic church because its concept of society is utterly foreign to Christian truth."[19] Now it was recognized, not only that it contained some positive elements but that with appropriate safeguards Christians might find it useful in their efforts to understand the world. López Trujillo had to be satisfied with this ambiguous disapproval. The theologians of liberation were relieved that in the negative climate of Puebla they had retained some legitimacy for the intellectual employment of Marxism.

At another point in the final document, Puebla addressed the theology of liberation directly and gave it formal approval. The theologians of liberation, it said, offer

an important service to the church. They systematize the doctrine and the directions of the magisterium in a synthesis with a more ample context, converting it into an idiom more suited to a given age. They subject the facts and the words revealed by God to new investigation in order to relate them to new sociocultural situations, or to new findings and problems raised by the sciences, history, or philosophy.[20]

Vatican Censure

López Trujillo got a formidable ally when in 1981 the German cardinal, Josef Ratzinger, was named head of the Vatican's Congregation for the Doctrine of the Faith. Ratzinger soon began to challenge the orthodoxy of the theology of liberation. In January 1984, *Oiga*, a Peruvian magazine, published a harsh attack on the theology of liberation, which it characterized as incompatible with the Christian faith. The article was anonymous, but it was twice reprinted over Ratzinger's name, in March in the Italian *30 Giorni*, organ of the conservative *Comunione e Liberazione* movement, and in August in the German *Neue Ordnung*. Ratzinger directed his severest criticisms against Gustavo Gutiérrez and Leonardo Boff, both of whom were the subject of investigation by the Congregation for the Doctrine of the Faith which ordered them to explain various positions they had expounded in their published works. Boff was forbidden to publish for a year. The Brazilian bishops, however, defended him, and the bishops of Peru similarly defended Gutiérrez. The affair ended without either side yielding.

Ratzinger's article in *Oiga*, *30 Giorni*, and *Neue Ordnung* was followed in the same year by the already mentioned *Instruction on Certain Aspects of the "Theology of Liberation."* In addition to its global condemnation of any theology that "tries to take" the Marxist analysis, this *Instruction* also challenged the dependency analysis. While recognizing the fact of extreme poverty, oppression, and "a mockery of elementary human rights" in many parts of Latin America, it blamed these conditions, not on social structures, but on the licentiousness and downright evil of individuals who played certain roles in those structures. The logic of the exposition was that the oppressed must suffer patiently until their oppressors are converted.

Ratzinger's 1984 document concluded by stating that it was concerned principally with the negative aspects of the theology of liberation and that a second statement would evaluate the positive aspects. This was done in April 1986 in a document entitled *Instruction Regarding Christian Liberty and Liberation*, widely said to have been written by Pope John Paul II himself.

It has something to say about a multitude of issues: ecology, decolonization, popular religiosity, self-determination, atheism, human rights, the preferential option for the poor, Christian base communities, the sense of faith of the people of God, relation of capital to work, reform and revolution, human promotion and evangelization, soteriological and socio-political liberation, progress on earth and the growth of the Kingdom.

While it reaffirms the generic warnings of Ratzinger's 1984 document, its final judgment can be summed up in words written a month later by John Paul in a letter to the bishops of Brazil:

The theology of liberation is not only opportune but useful and necessary. It should constitute a new phase — connected closely to those that preceded — of that theological reflexion begun with the Apostolic tradition and continued with the great Fathers and Doctors, with the church's ordinary and extraordinary magisterium, and in the most recent phase, with the rich patrimony of the social doctrine of the church expressed in documents that run from *Rerum Novarum* to *Laborem Exercens*.[21]

Clearly, Ratzinger did not win that round. On the contrary, John Paul II has accepted the theology of liberation as standing in the center of the Christian theological tradition.

The Protestants

No similar spectacular challenge occurred within the Protestant churches, not because the conflict was less deep, but because none of them has a centralized control of orthodoxy comparable to that of Rome. Perhaps the most publicized discussion took place in the United Methodist church in the United States when conservatives sought to force withdrawal from membership of the National Council of Churches on the ground that that body was identifying with and subsidizing Marxist causes. They argued their case both in the assemblies of the United Methodist church and in national media, including the *Reader's Digest.*

Similar charges were leveled against the World Council of Churches (WCC), mostly in the United States. The National Council of Churches was urged to withdraw from membership on the ground that the WCC was supporting such violent movements as the African National Congress. The Institute on Religion and Democracy, the Heritage Foundation, the American Enterprise Institute, and other research centers staffed by conservative intellectuals acquired a high visibility in the United States during the Reagan administration (1981–1989). They became the major, or at least the most visible, implementers of a recommendation regarding the theology of liberation contained in the Santa Fe document. Drawn up in 1980 as a program on Latin America for presidential candidate Ronald Reagan, this document asserted that the theology of liberation was opposed to the interests of the United States in the hemisphere. "U.S. foreign policy," it said, "must begin to counter (not react against) liberation theology as it is utilized in Latin America."[22] Nine years later the Santa Fe Committee repeated and expanded this advice for Reagan's successor as president, George Bush. Liberation theology, it asserted, is "a political doctrine disguised as religious belief." To combat "cultural" communist tendencies, it added, the United States should not concern itself primarily with "formal democratic processes," but rather rely on such traditional Latin American institutions as the armed forces, remembering that leftist opponents may be legitimately restrained in the interest of security and stability.[23]

•

Like the Christian base communities, whose reflection on their existential situation it abstracts and synthesizes, the theology of liberation survives with modest, not to say primitive, means. People who have no spare time because they are immersed in pastoral work among the poor produce it in their spare time. Yet, like the base communities, it continues to flourish against overwhelming odds. It is, in the summing up of Enrique Dussel, "a 'sign of the times,' the rich prophetic voice that creates the new; that which comes to move the people toward their historical and eschatological future, and that which appears to put into motion the dialectical movement of the countries which suffer from the neocolonial oppression of the North Atlantic empires."[24]

Conclusions

Dialogue has certainly not bridged over many of the gaps between the meaning and purpose of human existence as conceived by Christians and as conceived by Marxists. It has, nevertheless, clarified important areas of common commitment and dispelled not a few commonly held misrepresentations. Pride of place among these misrepresentations goes to the notion that Marxism is a single, indivisible system, claiming to contain the wholeness of truth, committed to serve unquestioningly the interests of Soviet Russia. Such indeed is the view that until recently was sedulously cultivated by the rulers of that state, and also by those of the United States. Not only can it no longer meet the test of observable fact, but the Russian leaders have themselves abandoned it since Mikhail Gorbachev came to power in the mid-1980s. Neither, indeed, can it stand up to the basic Marxist principle that Marxism is a scientific view of the world, since science is by definition experimental and thus susceptible to modification as new knowledge and new experiences change and correct its tentative conclusions.

Dialogue has focused principally on atheism and transcendence, two concepts the dialectical relationship of which is obvious. This is understandable, because atheism has been for Christians the most offensive aspect of Marxism, and transcendence has similarly been for Marxists one of the most objectionable elements of religious faith. Marxists reject the Christian belief that humanity will achieve its perfection only in the eschaton, when time and history end and all things are transformed in Christ. For them, humanity is destined to achieve its own perfection in this world.

Marxist philosopher Roger Garaudy, a leading participant in the dialogue, gives a description of the Marxist notion of atheism that is radically different from the popular understanding. Eighteenth-century atheism, he says, was essentially political. The Encyclopaedists and other Enlightenment thinkers found themselves in conflict with a church that was closely allied with an authoritarian and often tyrannical state. They fought religion as part of their effort to substitute democracy for absolute monarchy. Nineteenth-century atheism, apart from Marxism, was — still according to Garaudy — "scientist." It considered religious ideology to be a prescientific or nonscientific worldview. For Marx, however, and for twentieth-century atheists, according to Garaudy, atheism is essentially humanist. "It starts, not from a negation, but from an affirmation: it affirms the autonomy of man and it involves as a consequence the rejection of every attempt to rob man of his creative and self-creative power."[1]

Garaudy has returned frequently to the identification of the atheism of Marx as an affirmation of human autonomy. When Marx undertakes the critique of religion, he never does so in the name of a philosophical materialism; his critique is based on a historical analysis of the social contradictions and the ideological projections. What this means is that Marx never opposes an atheist assumption to a religious assumption. The reason is that both of them are outside the field of scientific problems. Marx had a clear understanding of the demands of scientific rigor. That is why he never fell into the error, so common among his successors, of claiming simultaneously for his teaching the status of a science and that of an ontology, a metaphysic, a pretended absolute knowledge of being. Science does not and cannot raise the metaphysical problems of materialism and of atheism: these are not scientific problems. All that science and Marxism can demand, if they wish to be scientific, is a "methodological atheism," that is, the refusal to make God either an "explanation" or a "force" intervening in the fabric of natural phenomena.[2] This does not necessarily make Marxism acceptable to the believer, but it conveys an image very different from that summoned up by the epithet "godless communism."[3]

Vitezslav Gardavsky (1923–), one of the most distinguished of Czech Marxist theoreticians, carries Garaudy's concept still farther. Himself a Jew, Gardavsky considers Marx's Jewish heritage very important in any attempt to understand him. The Jewish notion of humanity, as presented in the Bible in the story of the patriarch Jacob, he says, perceives the human as revolutionary potentiality. By wrestling with God, thus transcending all recognized boundaries, Jacob took charge of his own fate. His was "the first authentic human action." The significance of this line of argument is that for most Marxists Prometheus is the ultimate hero, the protagonist in the Greek myth who refused to submit to the domination of the gods. Not so, says Gardavsky. Greek mythology, as the story of Icarus shows, sets limits to what the human can achieve, whereas Hebrew mythology establishes no unpassable boundaries.[4]

Exactly the same contrast between the Promethean and the biblical understanding of the human potential is made by José María González Ruiz, a Spanish Catholic theologian.

A profound reading of the Bible led Paul Ricoeur to formulate this bold statement: "Unlike Greek wisdom Christianity does not condemn Prometheus: according to the Greeks, the 'sin' of Prometheus lies in having stolen fire, the fire of arts and crafts, the fire of knowledge and consciousness. The 'sin' of Adam, however, was not the same. Adam's disobedience was not in being a technical and knowing man, but in having broken the vital bond with the divine in his experience as man. Thus the first expression of that sin is the crime of Cain, the sin against his brother, not a sin against nature; the sin against love, not the sin against existence as an animal without history."

The biblical God is not presented as an immanent solution to the human and cosmic enigma. The scientific atheism of the century of the Enlightenment pretended to do without God because the God hypothesis was no longer necessary to explain the riddle of life. Throughout the Bible, on the contrary, God is presented as an unexplainable luxury. The divine presence is cosmic and human evolution is totally gratuitous. It cannot be grasped except through an explicit self-revelation by God himself. The biblical God breaks into the evolving reality of man under the total and absolute form of "grace" and the "gratuitous."

Paul explicitly affirms in the first two chapters of his letters to the Romans that in the Greco-Roman religious world the degradation of the gratuitous revelation of God has been brought about culpably in a theism manipulated by the interests of the ruling classes, "who by their wickedness suppress the truth" (Rom. 1:18). The name of God was sacred, and to speak it could accredit the position of a ruling group. For this reason, according to the Pauline analysis, it was necessary to reduce God to concrete and reachable dimensions, making him a part — although not the principal one — of the machinery of the cosmos and of society. From that moment on, God is involved in the farce of life. He becomes the jack-of-all-trades to solve all the doubts of the spirit and supply for all the deficiencies of mankind. This God-jack-of-all-trades gradually loses his functions as man illuminates with his own progress the shadowy zones of ignorance and impotence.... God's presence in the progressive evolution of man is a pure grace. It is something totally gratuitous.... It is a gratuitous gift which is not given to replace nature, let alone to rival it. Grace does not interfere with nature. It belongs to a different order and cannot be compared, either positively or negatively, with human nature.... Grace cannot be presented as a source of human alienation, for it neither rivals the laborious and progressive effort of humanity that takes place in historical evolution nor attempts to discourage men in this effort by presenting them with a prefabricated future fulfillment. Grace is not an intruder who is about to eclipse the epic grandeur of Prometheus.... The linking of man with god, as appears in the Bible, far from alienating him from his self-creative task, consists precisely in it. Man cannot give up his Promethean grandeur without automatically apostatizing from the God of Abraham, Isaac, and Jacob.... I would speak of an *eschatologizing* sense of history rather than an *eschatological* one. The eschatologization of the human adventure, far from demanding cessation of man's Promethean effort, is a stimulus and a guarantee of it ascending progress.[5]

While remaining an atheist, Gardavsky has gone beyond Garaudy in questioning the assumptions of atheists. It is as absurd for a communist not to believe as for a Christian to believe, he asserts. In addition, Marxism for him cannot hope to fulfil the functions that belief in God has traditionally fulfilled unless and until it "soaks up Christianity."[6] This comment has particular pertinence in the 1990s when socialist societies from the Soviet Union to Cuba are conscious of the revival of religious movements among their citizens and are seeking to identify the possible role of religion in promoting the social values that Marxism should theoretically have instilled but has not.

Christian participants in the dialogue freely acknowledge that it has helped them to clarify their understanding of God. They readily admit that humans tend to create their God in their own image and likeness. They agree with Marx to the extent that they recognize that the God widely worshiped in nineteenth-century

Europe and rejected by him was not the God of Jesus Christ. They also recognize that the characteristic of contemporary atheism is less a denial of God than an affirmation of the human. "It seems possible to speak of a positive characteristic common to all forms of contemporary atheism," writes Giulio Girardi.

Its central perspective always leads to man, not to God. Atheism shares the reflex, anthropological character of all modern thought. It poses, in its negative stage, more as a critique of religion than as a critique of God. God is thus considered primarily in relation to man. This relationship is not seen from God's point of view, however, but from man's point of view.[7]

The notion of transcendence has also been refined for Christians by the dialogue. Pierre Teilhard de Chardin, the Jesuit anthropologist and philosopher, had already pointed the way when he wrote: "The synthesis of the God of the Above and the God of the Ahead: this is the only God whom we shall in the future be able to adore in spirit and in truth."[8] Ernst Bloch, a Marxist who is particularly interested in eschatology, responds affirmatively to this approach. "If the salvation in the Gospel is to become flesh — for us or for men who follow — there must not be merely something above, but something before us."[9]

Marxists also are trying to deal with the notion of transcendence. At the Marienbad dialogue, described earlier, Gardavsky said that Christians and Marxists should be able to trust each other to bear responsibility for the future of the human race, or, as Christians would put it, "to work for the coming of God's kingdom." Pleading for a pluralism in Marxism, Professor Milan Pruha of the University of Prague said: "For a long time, we Marxists have tried to criticize and retard the Christian striving for transcendence. Should it not rather be our task to encourage Christians to be even more radical in striving for transcendence?" He added that Christians had even awakened in some Marxists "an appetite for transcendence."[10]

Roger Garaudy in a paraphrase of Teilhard concurs: "The synthesis of the God of the [Christian] Above and the [Marxist] God of the Ahead: this is the only God whom we shall in the future be able to adore in spirit and in truth."[11] Again, one must remain conscious of the ambiguity of words. If the "Ahead" of the Marxist is restricted to a historically immanent future, it still does not provide room for transcendence as understood by the Christian. There remains a gulf between Karl Rahner's transcendence as Absolute Future and Garaudy's future as a human creation, in itself simply a void.[12] Yet there may be room for a dialectic interconnection bridging the gulf between the two concepts. Dorothee Sölle is one who believes such a dialectic interconnection exists.

Unity is no longer conceived in dualist but in dialectical terms. In other words, the synthesis that we will find will not place in relationship an achieved faith and an achieved socialism. Both will transcend the level they have reached in the history of mankind until now: our praxis, by transcending what is given, will manifest "the truth — that is, reality and power, the historical rootedness of our thought."[13]

Notes

Preface

1. *The Random House Dictionary of the English Language* (New York: Random House, 1967).
2. *URSS oggi* (Agenzia Novosti, Via Chitunno 34, Rome) 18, nos. 21–22 (November 1989), pp. 12, 14, 51, 55.
3. Ibid.

Chapter 1: The Age-Old Socialist Dream

1. B. McGinn, *Apocalyptic Spirituality* (New York: Paulist Press, 1979), p. 100.
2. Adolfo Abascal-Jaen, "Christian Messianism or Apocalyptic Voluptuousness?" in *International Intercommunications*, Brussels, no. 40, Winter 1986–87.
3. Henri de Lubac, *La posterité spirituelle de Joachim de Fiore*, vol. 1 (Paris: Lethielleux, 1979).
4. Charles Avila, *Ownership* (Maryknoll, N.Y.: Orbis Books, 1983), pp. 86 and 120.
5. Bede Jarrett, *Medieval Socialism* (London: Burns, Oates & Washburn, 1935), p. 20; Thomas Aquinas, *Summa Theologica*, 2a, 2ae, 66, 2.
6. John C. Cort, *Christian Socialism* (Maryknoll, N.Y.: Orbis Books, 1988), pp. 101, 141; G. D. H Cole, *Socialist Thought: The Forerunners, 1789–1850* (London: MacMillan, 1953), p. 1.
7. Karl Marx and Friedrich Engels, *The Communist Manifesto*, with an Introduction by A. J. P. Taylor (Harmondsworth, Middlesex: Penguin, 1967), p. 62.
8. Roger Garaudy, *Marxism in the Twentieth Century* (London: Collins, 1970), p. 106.
9. Julius Braunthal, *History of the International*, vol. 1, 1864–1914 (New York: Praeger, 1967), p. 43.

10. A. Luciani, *Cristianesimo e movimento socialista in Europa*, vol. I,1, 1789–1848 (Venice: Marsilio Edizioni, 1984–1985), pp. 92–94.

11. A. W. Ward, G. W. Prothero, and Stanley Leathes, *The Cambridge Modern History* (Cambridge: University Press, 1907), p. 179.

12. Ercole Consalvi, *Mémoires du Cardinal Consalvi*, vol. 1 (Paris: Henri Plon, 1864), pp. 18ff.

13. Jean-Guy Vaillancourt, *Papal Power: A Study of Vatican Control over Lay Catholic Elites* (Berkeley: University of California Press, 1980), pp. 34ff.; Luciani, *Cristianesimo e movimento socialista in Europa*, vol. I,1, p. 94.

14. Karl Marx and Friedrich Engels, *The Communist Manifesto*.

15. Braunthal, *History of the International*, vol. 1, p. 43.

Chapter 2: *The Catholic Response*

1. Claudia Carlen, *The Papal Encyclicals*, I, 1740–1878 (Wilmington, N.C.: McGrath Publishing Co., 1981), 280, no. 16.

2. *LADOC* (Washington, D.C., U.S. Catholic Conference), IV, 1, September 1980.

3. Carlen, *The Papal Encyclicals*, I, 298, no. 18.

4. Ibid., I, 299, pars. 19–22.

5. *The Encyclical of Pope Pius IX and the Syllabus of Errors* (Baltimore: Kelly, Piet & Co., 1870), p. 16.

6. Julius Braunthal, *History of the International*, vol. 1, 1864–1914 (New York: Praeger, 1967), p. 157.

7. Ibid., p. 161.

8. *The Catholic Encyclopedia*, vol. 9 (New York: Appleton Co., 1907–1912) p. 169.

9. Carlen, *The Papal Encyclicals*, II, 1878–1903, 280, no. 16.

10. Ibid., nos. 18 and 19.

11. Ibid., 12, par. 1.

12. Jules Guesde, *Textes choisis, 1867–1882* (Paris: Les classiques du peuple, Editions Sociales, 1959), pp. 86–89.

13. *Rerum Novarum*, 15 and 19.

14. *Fin dalla prima*, December 18, 1903.

15. Par. 51, *The Catholic Mind* 37, no. 886 (November 22, 1939), p. 936.

16. Carlen, *The Papal Encyclicals*, III, 1903–1939, 432–33, pars. 111–113.

17. Ibid., 434, par. 117.

18. Ibid., 539, par. 9.

19. Karl Marx and Friedrich Engels, *Manifesto of the Communist Party* (Chicago: Charles H. Kerr, 1906), pp. 34–38

20. See Anselm K. Min, "The Vatican, Marxism, and Liberation Theology," *Cross Currents* 34, no. 4, p. 442.

Chapter 3: Utopian Socialists

1. A. Luciani, *Cristianesimo e movimento socialista in Europa*, vol. I,1, 1789–1848 (Venice: Marsilio Edizioni, 1984–1985), p. 41.

2. Ibid.

3. Charles E. Raven, *Christian Socialism 1848–1854* (London: Frank Cass & Co., 1968), p. 58.

4. John C. Cort, *Christian Socialism* (Maryknoll, N.Y.: Orbis Books, 1988), p. 140.

5. Warren Lerner, *A History of Socialism and Communism in Modern Times: Theorists, Activists, and Humanists* (Englewood Cliffs, N.J.: Prentice Hall, 1982), p. 60.

6. Peter d'A. Jones, *The Christian Socialist Revival, 1877–1914: Religion, Class, and Social Consciousness in Late-Victorian England* (Princeton, N.J.: Princeton University Press, 1968), p. 439.

7. Cort, *Christian Socialism*, p. 153.

8. Karl Marx and Friedrich Engels. *The Communist Manifesto*, with an Introduction by A. J. P. Taylor (Harmondsworth, Middlesex: Penguin, 1967), p. 108.

9. *Asce-News* 11/12–1979, p. 42.

10. Ronald Preston, "Christian Socialism Becalmed," *Theology* 91 (January 1988), pp. 24–32.

11. Luciani, *Cristianesimo e movimento socialista in Europa*, vol. I,1, pp. 194–195.

12. Quoted by Dorothee Sölle in *Cross Currents*, Winter 1975, p. 419.

13. Luciani, *Cristianesimo e movimento socialista in Europa*, vol. I,2, 1848–1890, p. 528.

14. Ibid., p. 530.

15. James Bentley, *Between Marx and Christ: The Dialogue in German-Speaking Europe, 1870–1970* (London: Verso Editions and NLB, 1982), p. 62.

16. Luciani, *Cristianesimo e movimento socialista in Europa*, vol. II,2, 1890–1945, p. 342.

17. Henry F. May, *Protestant Churches and Industrial America* (New York: Harper & Row, 1949), p. 235. I am deeply indebted for this survey of Protestant involvement in the United States to Robert Hedborg Craig's doctoral dissertation (Columbia University, 1975), "Seek Ye First the Political Kingdom: Socialism in the United States, 1890–1920."

18. Walter Rauschenbusch, *Christianizing the Social Order* (New York: Macmillan, 1912), pp. 403–405.

19. *Christian Socialist* 3 (July 1, 1906), p. 4. Quoted by Craig, "Seek Ye First the Political Kingdom."

20. Rauschenbusch, *Christianizing the Social Order*, pp. 40ff.

21. *Christian Socialist* 4 (May 15, 1907).

22. *International Socialist Review* 1 (January 1901), p. 34, quoted by Craig, "Seek Ye First the Political Kingdom."

23. Mari Jo Buhle, *Women and American Socialism, 1870–1920* (Chicago: University of Illinois Press, 1981), p. 81.

24. Cort, *Christian Socialism*, p. 262.

25. James Weinstein, *The Decline of Socialism in America, 1912–1925* (New York: Monthly Review Press, 1967), pp. 53–56.

26. Howard Zinn, *A People's History of the United States* (New York: Harper & Row, 1980), pp. 346–349.

27. H. Richard Niebuhr, *Christ and Culture* (New York: Harper & Row, 1956).

28. Fyodor Mikhailovich Dostoevsky, *The Brothers Karamazov* (Chicago: Encyclopaedia Britannica, 1952), p. 32.

29. *The Nation* 241, no. 1 (July 6–13, 1985), p. 12.

Chapter 4: Christians for Socialism

1. Quoted in *Latinamerica Press* (*Noticias Aliadas*), Lima, Peru, December 20, 1973.

2. *Facts on File* 16, no. 799, 1-5-21 February 1974; Seweryn Bialer, *Stalin's Successors* (New York: Cambridge University Press, 1980), p. 103.

3. Rafael Avila, "Chronology of the Theology of Liberation and Revolutionary Christians in Latin America," *Latinamerica Press*, December 13, 1973, p. 5.

4. Gary MacEoin, *Revolution Next Door: Latin America in the 1970s* (New York: Holt, Rinehart & Winston, 1971), pp. 81ff. and 107ff.

5. Deane William Ferm, *Third World Liberation Theologies: A Reader* (Maryknoll, N.Y.: Orbis Books, 1986), p. 5; the phrase quoted is from *Populorum Progressio*, no. 26.

6. *Populorum Progressio*, no. 76.

7. Ferm, *Third World Liberation Theologies: A Reader*, pp. 7–8.

8. Ives Vaillancourt, "The Crisis of ILADES," in *Social-Activist Priests in Chile*, LADOC "Keyhole" Series, no. 5, Washington D.C., U.S. Catholic Conference, p. 9.

9. Ferm, *Third World Liberation Theologies: A Reader*, pp. 12.

10. *Mensaje* (Santiago, Chile) 21, no. 206 (January–February 1972), p. 57; *Christians for Socialism* (Washington, D.C.: EPICA, 1973), pp. 4–10 and 13–15.

11. *Los cristianos y el socialismo*, I Encuentro latinoamericano (Buenos Aires: Siglo XXI, 1973), pp. 18–19.

12. Instituto de Estudios Políticos, 1972, p. 161.

13. *Vida Nueva* (Madrid), January 25, 1977.

14. A. Luciani, *Cristianesimo e movimento socialista in Europa*, vol. III, 1945–1985 (Venice: Marsilio Edizioni, 1984–1985), p. 468.

15. Avila, Bologna, and Burgos documents in *Option for Struggle II*, Church Research and Information Projects, Box 223, Cathedral Station, New York, NY 10025, 1975. Naples document in *Cristiani per il socialismo: atti del Secondo Convegno Nazionale*, November 14, 1974, Pistoia, Italy, 1975.

16. *Option for Struggle II*.

Chapter 5: Christian-Marxist Dialogue in Europe

1. Girardi, Giulio, *Marxism and Christianity* (Dublin: Gill & Macmillan, 1968), p. viii.

2. Paolo Filo della Torre, Edward Mortimer, and Jonathan Story, eds. *Eurocommunism: Myth or Reality?* (Middlesex, England: Penguin, 1979), p. 9.

3. Ibid., pp. 15 and 74.

4. Ibid., p. 78.

5. Text of Bettazzi letter and Berlinguer reply in *Documentation "Euro-dialogue,"* Bulletin no. 4, IDOC International new series, Rome, April 1978, pp. 3–7 and 16–18.

6. *La politica e l'organizzazione dei comunisti italiani: Le tesi e lo statuto approvati dal XV Congresso Nazionale del PCI* (Roma: Editori Reuniti, 1979), Thesis no. 14.

7. *Documentation "Eurodialogue,"* Bulletin no. 4, pp. 10–11.

8. Filo della Torre, *Eurocommunism: Myth or Reality?* p. 176.

9. Text of Declaration, dated November 15, 1975, in ibid., pp. 334–338.

10. Filo della Torre, *Eurocommunism: Myth or Reality?* pp. 15 and 93.

11. James Bentley, *Between Marx and Christ: The Dialogue in German-Speaking Europe, 1870–1970* (London: Verso Editions and NLB, 1982), p. 81.

12. Ernst Bloch, *The Principle of Hope* (Oxford: Basil Blackwell, 1986), p. 158.

13. Jürgen Moltmann, *Religion, Revolution, and the Future* (New York: Charles Scribner's Sons, 1969), p. 15.

14. Jürgen Moltmann, *Theology of Hope: On the Ground and the Implications of a Christian Eschatology* (London: SCM Press, 1967), p. 338.

15. Bentley, *Between Marx and Christ*, pp. 144–145; Peter Hebble-

thwaite, *The Christian-Marxist Dialogue* (London: Darton, Longman & Todd, 1977), p. 17.

16. *New Blackfriars* 61, no. 720 (May 1980), p. 240.

17. Roger Garaudy, *From Anathema to Dialogue: The Challenge of Marxist-Christian Cooperation* (London: Collins, 1967), p. 83.

18. Ibid., p. 11.

19. Ibid., p. 111.

20. *Cross Currents* 25, no. 4 (Winter 1975), pp. 419–420.

21. Postscript to Girardi in French edition, Paris, 1968, p. 303.

22. José Míguez Bonino, *Christians and Marxists: The Mutual Challenge to Revolution* (London: Hodder & Stoughton, 1976), pp. 16 and 29.

Chapter 6: Theology of Liberation

1. *Iglesia Viva* (Madrid), nos. 116–117, March–June 1985.

2. Rosino Gibellini, *The Liberation Theology Debate* (Maryknoll, N.Y.: Orbis Books, 1988), p. 2. Gibellini further subdivides the formative phase into a euphoric period until 1972, followed by a period of "captivity and exile."

3. Hugo Assmann, *Theology for a Nomad Church* (Maryknoll, N.Y.: Orbis Books, 1976), p. 129.

4. For a discussion of the dependency theory, see Robert Gilpin, *The Political Economy of International Relations* (Princeton: Princeton University Press, 1987), pp. 181–191.

5. *Cristianismo y Sociedad* (Montevideo), no. 84, 1985. Gibellini, *The Liberation Theology Debate*, p. 13.

6. Gibellini, *The Liberation Theology Debate*, p. 18.

7. *Jeevadhara: A Journal of Christian Interpretation*, no. 90 (November 1985), p. 480.

8. Text of Instruction in Juan Luis Segundo, *Theology and the Church* (London: Geoffrey Chapman, 1985), pp. 169–188; quotation, p. 177.

9. Ibid., p. 96.

10. *Cross Currents* 34, no. 4 (Winter 1984–1985), p. 442. Italics in original.

11. Gregory Baum, *The Priority of Labor* (New York: Paulist Press, 1982), p. 3.

12. Karl Lehmann, *Theologie der Befreiung* (Einsiedeln: Johannes Verlag, 1977), p. 180.

13. Enrique Dussel, *A History of the Church in Latin America: From Colonialism to Liberation, 1492–1979* (Grand Rapids Mich.: William B. Eerdmans, 1981), p. 327.

14. December 1971 Vekemans request to Misereor for funds "for the study of this phenomenon in the Latin American church."

15. *LADOC* (Washington, D.C.), U.S.C.C., no. 60, September–October 1975.

16. *Cross Currents* 27, no. 1 (Spring 1978). Gary MacEoin and Nivita Riley, *Puebla: A Church Being Born* (New York: Paulist Press, 1979), pp. 54–63.

17. John Eagleson and Philip Scharper, eds., *Puebla and Beyond* (Maryknoll, N.Y.: Orbis Books, 1979), par. 544, p. 200.

18. Michael Walsh and Brian Davies, eds., *Documents from John XXIII to John Paul II* (London: Collins, 1984), p. 178.

19. Claudia Carlen, *The Papal Encyclicals*, III, 1903–1939 (Wilmington, N.C.: McGrath Publishing Co., 1981), p. 434, no. 16.

20. Par. 375, in Eagleson and Scharper, eds., *Puebla and Beyond*, p. 176.

21. *Revista Eclesiastica Brasileira* 46, no. 182 (June 1986), p. 400.

22. Committee of Santa Fe, 1980, p. 20.

23. *Latinamerica Press*, Lima, Peru, January 5, 1989, p. 3.

24. Enrique Dussel, *History and the Theology of Liberation: A Latin American Perspective* (Maryknoll, N.Y.: Orbis Books, 1976), p. 255.

Conclusions

1. Roger Garaudy, *Marxism in the Twentieth Century* (London: Collins, 1970), p. 107.

2. Roger Garaudy, *Reconquête de l'espoir* (Paris: Editions Bernard Grasset, 1971), p. 124.

3. See Russell Bradner Norris, *God, Marx, and the Future: A Dialogue with Roger Garaudy* (Philadelphia: Fortress Press, 1974), p. 28.

4. James Bentley, *Between Marx and Christ: The Dialogue in German-Speaking Europe, 1870–1970* (London: Verso Editions and NLB, 1982), pp. 142–143.

5. José María González Ruiz, *Atheistic Humanism and the Biblical God* (Milwaukee: Bruce, 1969), pp. 14ff.

6. Bentley, *Between Marx and Christ*, p. 144.

7. Giulio Girardi, *Marxism and Christianity* (Dublin: Gill & Macmillan, 1968), p. 9.

8. Roger Garaudy, *From Anathema to Dialogue: The Challenge of Marxist-Christian Cooperation* (London: Collins, 1967), p. 46.

9. Ernst Bloch, "Man as Possibility," *Cross Currents* 18, no. 3 (Summer 1968), p. 283. Johannes B. Metz, "God Before Us Instead of a Theological Argument," *Cross Currents*, 18, no. 3 (Summer 1968), pp. 296–306.

10. Bentley, *Between Marx and Christ*, p. 145.

11. Garaudy, *From Anathema to Dialogue*, p. 54.

12. See Norris, *God, Marx, and the Future*, p. 195.

13. "Christians for Socialism," *Cross Currents*, 25, no. 4 (Winter 1975), p. 434. The citation is from Marx's *Second Thesis on Feuerbach*.

Bibliography

Abbott, Walter M., ed. *The Documents of Vatican II*. New York: Guild Press, 1966.

Alves, Rubem. *A Theology of Human Hope*. Washington, D.C.: Corpus Books, 1969.

Aptheker, Herbert. *The Urgency of Marxist-Christian Dialogue*. New York: Harper & Row, 1970.

Assmann, Hugo. *Theology for a Nomad Church*. Maryknoll, N.Y.: Orbis Books, 1976.

Avila, Charles. *Ownership*. Maryknoll, N.Y.: Orbis Books, 1983.

Avinieri, Shlomo. *The Social and Political Thought of Karl Marx*. Cambridge, England: Cambridge University Press, 1968.

Baudry, Gerard-Henry. *Socialisme et Humanisme: Emmanuel Mounier, Teilhard de Chardin*. Lille: G.-H. Baudry, 1978.

Baum, Gregory. *The Priority of Labor*. New York: Paulist Press, 1982.

Bentley, James. *Between Marx and Christ: The Dialogue in German-Speaking Europe, 1870–1970*. London: Verso Editions and NLB, 1982.

Berryman, Phillip. *The Religious Roots of Rebellion: Christians in Central American Revolutions*. Maryknoll, N.Y.: Orbis Books, 1984.

———. *Liberation Theology*. Oak Park, Ill.: Meyer-Stone Books, 1987.

Bialer, Seweryn. *Stalin's Successors*. New York: Cambridge University Press, 1980.

Bloch, Ernst. *Atheism in Christianity*. New York: Herder & Herder, 1972.

———. *The Principle of Hope*. Oxford: Basil Blackwell, 1986.

Boff, Leonardo. *Jesus Christ Liberator*. Maryknoll, N.Y.: Orbis Books, 1978.

———, and Clodovis Boff. *Introducing Liberation Theology*. Maryknoll, N.Y.: Orbis Books, 1988.

Braunthal, Julius. *History of the International*. Vol. 1, 1864–1914; vol. 2, 1914–1943. New York: Praeger, 1967. Vol. 3, 1943–1968. Old Westbury, Conn.: Westview, 1980.

Buhle, Mari Jo. *Women and American Socialism, 1870–1920.* Chicago: University of Illinois Press, 1981.

Calvez, Jean-Ives, and Jacques Perrin. *The Church and Social Justice: the Social Teachings of the Popes from Leo XIII to Pius XII (1878–1958).* London: Burns and Oates, 1961.

Carlen, Claudia. *The Papal Encyclicals.* I, 1740–1878; II, 1878–1903; III, 1903–1939; IV, 1939–1958; V, 1958–1981. Wilmington, N.C.: McGrath Publishing Co., 1981.

The Catholic Encyclopedia, 15 vols. New York: Appleton Co., 1907–1912.

Cole, G. D. H. *Socialist Thought: The Forerunners, 1789–1850.* London: MacMillan, 1953.

Committee of Santa Fe. *A New Inter-American Policy for the Eighties.* Washington, D.C.: Inter-American Security Council, 1980.

Consalvi, Ercole. *Mémoires du Cardinal Consalvi.* Paris: Henri Plon, 1864.

Cort, John C. *Christian Socialism.* Maryknoll, N.Y.: Orbis Books, 1988.

Dostoevsky, Fyodor Mikhailovich. *The Brothers Karamazov.* Chicago: Encyclopaedia Britannica, 1952.

Dussel, Enrique. *History and the Theology of Liberation: A Latin American Perspective.* Maryknoll, N.Y.: Orbis Books, 1976.

───. *A History of the Church in Latin America: From Colonialism to Liberation, 1492–1979.* Grand Rapids Mich.: William B. Eerdmans, 1981.

Eagleson, John, and Philip Scharper, eds., *Puebla and Beyond.* Maryknoll, N.Y.: Orbis Books, 1979.

Ferm, Deane William. *Third World Liberation Theologies: A Reader.* Maryknoll, N.Y.: Orbis Books, 1986.

Fever, Lewis S., ed. *Basic Writings on Politics and Philosophy: Karl Marx and Friedrich Engels.* New York: Doubleday-Anchor, 1959.

Filo della Torre, Paolo, Edward Mortimer, and Jonathan Story, eds. *Eurocommunism: Myth or Reality?* Middlesex, England: Penguin, 1979.

Garaudy, Roger. *From Anathema to Dialogue: The Challenge of Marxist-Christian Cooperation.* London: Collins, 1967.

───. *Marxism in the Twentieth Century.* London: Collins, 1970.

───. *Reconquête de l'espoir.* Paris: Editions Bernard Grasset, 1971.

───. *Appel aux Vivants.* Paris: Editions du Seuil, 1979.

Gibellini, Rosino. *The Liberation Theology Debate.* Maryknoll, N.Y.: Orbis Books, 1988.

Girardi, Giulio. *Marxism and Christianity.* Dublin: Gill & Macmillan, 1968.

Group of Eighty. *Christians for Socialism.* Washington, D.C.: EPICA, 1973.

Guesde, Jules. *Textes choisis, 1867–1882.* Paris: Les classiques du peuple, Editions Sociales, 1959.

Gutiérrez, Gustavo. *A Theology of Liberation*. Maryknoll, N.Y.: Orbis Books, 1973.

Hebblethwaite, Peter. *The Christian-Marxist Dialogue*. London: Darton, Longman & Todd, 1977.

Hinkelammert, Franz J. *The Ideological Weapons of Death: A Theological Critique of Capitalism*. Maryknoll, N.Y.: Orbis Books, 1986.

Instituto de Estudios Políticos. *¿Consecuencia cristiana o alienación política?* Santiago de Chile: Editorial del Pacífico, 1972.

Jones, Peter d'A. *The Christian Socialist Revival, 1877–1914: Religion, Class, and Social Consciousness in Late-Victorian England*. Princeton, N.J.: Princeton University Press, 1968.

Lash, Nicholas. *A Matter of Hope: A Theologian's Reflections on the Thought of Karl Marx*. London: Darton, Longman & Todd, 1981.

Lehmann, Karl. *Theologie der Befreiung*. Einsiedeln: Johannes Verlag, 1977.

Lerner, Warren. *A History of Socialism and Communism in Modern Times: Theorists, Activists, and Humanists*. Englewood Cliffs, N.J.: Prentice Hall, 1982.

Lubac, Henri de. *La postérité spirituelle de Joachim de Flore*. 2 vols. Paris: Lethielleux, 1979, 1981.

Luciani, A. *Cristianesimo e movimento socialista in Europa*. Vol. I,1, 1789–1848; vol. I,2, 1848–1890; vol. II, 1 and 2, 1890–1945; vol. III, 1945–1985. Venice: Marsilio Edizioni, 1984–1985.

MacEoin, Gary. *Revolution Next Door: Latin America in the 1970s*. New York: Holt, Rinehart & Winston, 1971.

McGinn, B. *Apocalyptic Spirituality*. New York: Paulist Press, 1979.

McLellan, D. *Marxism and Religion*. San Francisco: Harper & Row, 1987.

————, and Nivita Riley. *Puebla: A Church Being Born*. New York: Paulist Press, 1979.

Marx Karl. *Capital, the Communist Manifesto, and Other Writings*. New York: Modern Library, 1932.

————, and Friedrich Engels. *Manifesto of the Communist Party*. Chicago: Charles H. Kerr, 1906.

————, and Friedrich Engels. *The Communist Manifesto*, with an Introduction by A. J. P. Taylor. Harmondsworth, Middlesex: Penguin, 1967.

May, Henry F. *Protestant Churches and Industrial America*. New York: Harper & Row, 1949.

Míguez Bonino, José. *Christians and Marxists: The Mutual Challenge to Revolution*. London: Hodder & Stoughton, 1976.

Miranda, José Porfirio. *Marx and the Bible: A Critique of the Philosophy of Oppression*. Maryknoll, N.Y.: Orbis Books, 1974.

Moltmann, Jürgen. *Theology of Hope: On the Ground and the Implications of a Christian Eschatology*. London: SCM Press, 1967.

————. *Religion, Revolution, and the Future*. New York: Charles Scribner's Sons, 1969.

————, Herbert W. Richardson, Johann Baptist Metz, Willi Oelmüller, and M. Darrol Bryant. *Religion and Political Society*. New York: Harper & Row, 1974.

New Catholic Encyclopedia. New York: Catholic University, 1967.

Niebuhr, H. Richard. *Christ and Culture*. New York: Harper & Row, 1956.

Norris, Russell Bradner. *God, Marx, and the Future: A Dialogue with Roger Garaudy*. Philadelphia: Fortress Press, 1974.

Raines, John C., and Thomas Dean, eds. *Marxism and Radical Religion: Essays Toward a Revolutionary Humanism*. Philadelphia: Temple University Press, 1970.

Rauschenbusch, Walter. *Christianizing the Social Order*. New York: Macmillan, 1912.

Raven, Charles E. *Christian Socialism 1848–1854*. London: Frank Cass & Co., 1968.

Segundo, Juan Luis. *Theology and the Church*. London: Geoffrey Chapman, 1985.

Vaillancourt, Jean-Guy. *Papal Power: A Study of Vatican Control over Lay Catholic Elites*. Berkeley: University of California Press, 1980.

Walsh, Michael, and Brian Davies, eds. *Documents from John XXIII to John Paul II*. London: Collins, 1984.

Ward, A. W., G. W. Prothero, and Stanley Leathes. *The Cambridge Modern History*. Cambridge: University Press, 1907.

Weinstein, James. *The Decline of Socialism in America, 1912–1925*. New York: Monthly Review Press, 1967.

Wilmore, Gayraud S., and James H. Cone. *Black Theology: A Documentary History, 1966–1979*. Maryknoll, N.Y.: Orbis Books, 1986.

Zinn, Howard. *A People's History of the United States*. New York: Harper & Row, 1980.

Index